TRAP-LINES NORTH

TRAP-LINES NORTH

A TRUE STORY OF THE CANADIAN WOODS

By

STEPHEN W. MEADER

ILLUSTRATED

DODD, MEAD AND COMPANY
NEW YORK   1966

ISBN 1-931177-06-6 cloth
ISBN 1-931177-07-4 paperback

SOUTHERN SKIES

LITTLE ROCK, ARKANSAS

Dedication

The republication of this book is dedicated to Lane Kidd by his old hunting buddy, Jerry Atchley.

Fisher

FOREWORD

Dᴉᴅ you ever wish, when you were reading a story about Daniel Boone, or Kit Carson, or Davy Crockett, that you could meet the hero face to face? Talk with him—hunt and travel with him—spread your blankets beside his, under the wilderness stars?

A few weeks ago it was my privilege to do something very like that. Early this spring two small notebooks in oilcloth covers came to me in the mail. They were stained and dog-eared, spotted with candle grease, smudged with wood smoke. They were filled with laborious pencil scrawls—laconic daily entries in the form of a diary that covered a period of seven months—from October 10, 1932 to May 20, 1933.

That was my introduction to Jim Vanderbeck. The diary was sent me by a friend of the Vanderbeck family, who had hunted and fished the virgin country north of Thunder Bay with Jim and his father.

I read the two little notebooks that night with a mounting glow of excitement. Here were the real experiences of an eighteen-year-old boy in an environment as primitive as any that Boone and Crockett knew. Brief and matter-of-fact as his jottings were, they caught my imagination with vivid, homely phrases that reeked of the pioneer North. Many of them were written by feeble candlelight after days of back-breaking work in sub-Arctic temperatures.

I wanted to know this youngster.

Early in June came his letter saying he would have a week free when we could go off on a canoe trip together. And on Sunday evening, June 15, I climbed down from the Canadian National's Continental Limited in Nakina.

Nakina lies northeast of Lake Nipigon, and 150 miles due north of Lake Superior. It takes two days and a night to reach the town by rail from New York, but the trip is worth it. All day Sunday, on the run northwest from Capreol, I had sat in the observation car and watched the endless panorama of the bush unfold. At intervals of an hour or so, the long train would stop at a tiny board station. A few log huts clustered beside the track, a white-painted Hudson's Bay Post, a handful of stolid faced Indians and a noisy gathering of big mongrel dogs made up the foreground. Behind them stretched the forest, untamed and measureless.

Jim met me on the platform at Nakina. A big, sunburned boy, shy at first but quickly at his ease. We walked up the track to the story-and-a-half log house that is the Vanderbecks' summer home, and there I was introduced to the rest of the family.

They were a stalwart crew, full of plain woods sense and ready laughter. After the first reserve had worn off, I was accepted as a friend. And in the North, friendship is no empty term. I could understand, as I listened to the talk that went round, how such a family would take adversity with a grin. They had known hard times and were working their way out.

Mrs. Vanderbeck supervised the packing of our supplies next morning. She must have thought this tenderfoot had a hungry look, for the green-painted grub box was bursting with nearly eighty pounds of food. We loaded our outfit on the truck and were set down on the shore of Cordingley Lake, where the Vanderbeck canoes are racked up. Young Lindsay and the driver waved us a farewell, and theirs were the last human faces we saw till our return, five days later.

Fortunately for my unskilled muscles, we took things easily that first day, camping at a big ledge on Poplar Lake. It was the mosquito season, but a chilly east wind kept them off, and we sat by the camp fire with real enjoyment. Our tent was tight and had a net across the front. Snug in our eiderdowns, we slept luxuriously till broad daylight.

I soon found that Jim was the best woods cook in my experience. With characteristic modesty he said anybody could cook if they had good provisions, and certainly ours were of the best. There were three dozen fresh eggs, in a bulky cardboard box which had a habit of catching twigs on the portages. There was excellent tinned butter, Canadian bacon, real North woods maple syrup for the flapjacks, a fine brand of American coffee, English marmalade, fresh vegetables and canned fruits.

I expostulated. This wasn't the Spartan fare I had expected—the winter ration Jim had known on his trap-line.

The boy laughed at me. "Ma wanted me to feed you right," he said. "This is the regular grub we give our parties of sportsmen, and they don't complain. Besides, you'd never make it over the long portage, if all you'd had for breakfast was tea and dried moose meat." And a few hours later, panting at the end of the mile-and-three-quarters carry, I was ready to admit he was right.

That was the only clear, warm day we had on the trip. Jim explained that it took good weather to drive the moose out of the bush and into the water—their favorite refuge from the flies. For that reason he confidently predicted we would see a moose that morning, and advised me to have the camera ready. Sure enough, as we slipped down a winding thoroughfare between two ponds, we sighted a big black bull, chest-deep among the lily stems. He waded ashore after a casual glance at us, and went off into the woods. But I had snapped him twice before he disappeared.

We reached Wababimiga a little after noon and faced a white-cap breeze that whipped up the full stretch of the open lake, dead against us. Two hours of hard driving with the paddles brought us in sight of the Vanderbecks' winter cabin. I could see at once why all of them loved this place—the stout log house set well back in its green clearing—the tall balm of gilead trees by the water—the white crescent of beach curving along the shore.

We spent two nights in that idyllic setting. The days were cold and cloudy with an occasional drizzle of rain, but we filled the time with talk and with work on a map of Jim's trapping country. The only interruptions were for meals and a couple of forays

FOREWORD

down a nearby river. I thought I had seen good-sized
brook trout, but the monsters that leaped in those
pools and rapids left me goggle-eyed. Jim spoke off-
handedly of an eight-pounder caught the year before.
The biggest one we landed was a fighting beauty that
weighed a bit over four pounds and measured 21
inches—just an everage trout in those waters.

Much of the family's winter gear is stored at Waba,
and I spent hours examining homemade toboggans,
canoe-sleds, caribou-hide moccasins and sealskin mukluks. Jim showed me how snowshoe frames are
worked into shape, and how the filling is woven from
strips of raw moose hide. We discussed trap sets and
stretchers, sled dogs and dog harness.

Jim had a man's sure knowledge of these things,
and a patience in explaining them that won my un-
bounded respect. At other times, when we talked
about the life of cities and my own business of writing, he was just a boy, wide-eyed with curiosity.

Once, at night, as we lay in the tent with the wind
roaring above us, he told me how his family name
came to Canada—almost an epic in itself. It was a
hundred years ago that Jim's great-grandfather migrated from the Dutch settlements of the Hudson
Valley to the province of New Brunswick. The
youngest member of the family was a newborn baby
boy. The Vanderbecks found a place that suited them
near the Restigouche River and set about clearing a

homestead. But before they were well settled came the great Restigouche fire, still talked about in the maritime provinces. Thousands of square miles of forest burned. As the flames swept nearer the Vanderbeck cabin, the father made a little brush raft, tied the eight-months-old infant upon it, and placed it in the swift current of the river. Next day the raft was picked up many miles downstream by people who knew the baby's name. He was unharmed, and lived to found the New Brunswick family of which Jim's is the third generation.

Our return trip to Nakina was uneventful except for almost running over a mother wood duck and her convoy of eleven fuzzy babies. We gave the mother the satisfaction of luring our canoe away from the brood, which she accomplished by a great quacking and fluttering along the water.

Thursday night we camped in the rain at the top of High Hill Portage. The tent was pitched squarely in the middle of a broad moose trail running along the crown of the ridge. There was moose sign everywhere, but the animals themselves kept out of sight. As we threaded the thoroughfares, next morning, I watched vainly with the camera at every bend. Once we saw bits of pulled grass floating and heard a distant crash in the undergrowth. The moist wind had carried our scent before us.

Moose are an important factor in the Vanderbecks'

livelihood. There is probably no finer moose country on the continent than along these northward-flowing rivers, beyond the height of land. And hunters who know it are beginning to make the journey to Nakina.

At the end of the Long Portage I picked up a big cone of birch bark, cunningly fashioned. It was a horn used by Jim's father—a famous moose-caller—during last fall's hunting. Autographed and hung in a place of honor, it now adorns my son's room at home.

We left our duffel on the lake shore and walked the three miles into town, the thought of a hot bath and a change into dry clothes quickening our pace. "Big Lindsay" Vanderbeck met us at the storehouse, grinning a welcome.

"Jim give you enough to eat?" was his first question. I praised the young guide's ability as a cook, but he remained unconvinced. "Come up to the house tonight and taste some *real* cooking," he urged.

Dinner that night was a state occasion, as I realized when I saw Jim in store clothes, his hair neatly parted and slicked down. Mrs. Vanderbeck and Ida had performed prodigies in the kitchen. I did my best with the mountains of meat and vegetables they set before me, but was finally vanquished by the second piece of cake. Jim, young Lindsay and I strolled out into the sunset to recuperate and feed the dogs.

FOREWORD

Old Bruno, Pat, Mutt, Brownie and the rest were hurling themselves to the length of their chains—panting, whining with eagerness. They had no idea of posing for their portraits, but I managed to get two or three snapshots—from a safe distance.

Jim showed me his vegetable garden, where the neat rows were already sprouting green. Few people in Nakina attempt to raise vegetables, for there are quite likely to be snowstorms in early June, and killing frosts may be expected before the end of August. However, the Finlanders are used to such summers, and Jim has been the apt pupil of a Finnish homesteader living close by. For several years the Vanderbecks have been able to provision their parties with fresh garden truck—an almost unheard-of luxury in that part of Canada.

My visit ended with an evening of story-telling and laughter in the cozy living room where these very genuine people entertained me. Boxes full of photographs were brought out for my inspection. Long yarns about wolves and Indians, blizzards and "Mounties" were spun.

In the morning Jim and his father came to the train to see me off. My luggage and the big bark moose-horn were stowed in the seat and the sincerity of the handshakes that followed left my fingers numb.

"Come back soon!" they called, as the Limited got

under way. And as I look back on the experiences of that Northland week, I think I shall take them at their word.

*   *   *   *

In most details, "Trap-Lines North" faithfully follows Jim's diary. It comes as near being a true story as any yarn you are likely to read. Occasionally I have put in incidents which happened in other winters of the boys' trapping, or in the lives of their close friends. But as far as I know none of the facts have been distorted. If you go up to Nakina any time after the first of November, and travel north with a dog sled, you'll find the same hardy youngsters mushing along the snowy trails and making their winter's living.

STEPHEN W. MEADER

September, 1935

TRAP-LINES NORTH

Marten

I

THE wind had a bite to it. Jim turned the collar of
his mackinaw high as he headed westward up the
track. Lights had begun to blink in the windows of
the settlement huddled beside the rails, but overhead
the cold immensity of the northern twilight still
veiled the stars.

At seven o'clock half of Nakina's six hundred people would be down at the station to see the Continental Limited come in. Now they were inside their
warm log houses, cooking and waiting for supper.
The rustle of that small wind from the north was
all that broke the stillness.

[1]

Jim walked the ties without seeing them. His thoughts were away in the bush. It was only three days since he had come in with the season's last party —a well-fed New Yorker and his two sons, who had gone home happy, with their moose head in the baggage car. But already he was restless. The sharp frosts of September had long since stripped the hardwoods, and there was a skim of ice each morning on the pools beside the track. An inch or two of snow had fallen, that first week of October. Winter was near.

A faint, far sound in the silence made the boy pause, lifting his head. It came once more, thin and clear—the honk of a Canada goose. Across the pale depths of the evening sky he saw a wedge of dark wings cutting southward. The flocks of pintails and green-winged teal, the mallards and golden-eyes, had begun the journey weeks before. When the big gray geese flew south it meant the end of open water. Jim drew a long breath and quickened his stride. He was grinning when he reached the log house and opened the door.

"Hey, Lindsay," he called.

His chunky sixteen-year-old brother was curled up by the lamp with a magazine. "Don't bother me," he grunted. But Jim made a dive for him and tousled his blond hair.

"Listen, lazybones," he said, "another two weeks and there'll be ice on the lakes. You know how much we've got to do while we can still use the canoes, and I bet you haven't got half your outfit together."

"Huh!" grunted Lindsay. "I'll be ready when you are. Go on, now, and let me finish this. It's a darn good detective story."

Jim washed in the basin at the sink and sniffed hungrily at the waves of fragrance wafted from the stove.

"What've you got for supper, Ma?"

Mrs. Vanderbeck wiped her warm, ruddy face with a corner of her apron. She was a big woman and she walked with a solid authority, but she could move fast when a meal was in the making.

"Hush now, boy, and see that you're ready when the food's on the table," she answered gently. "Whatever it is you can be grateful, with things the way they are."

Jim nodded and there were sober lines about his mouth as he returned to the front room. The sheet-iron stove radiated a comfortable heat, and the log walls, oakum chinked, gave back the warmth. The boy sprawled on the couch in the corner, and taking a thumb-worn letter out of his pocket, reread it for the twentieth time. It was from his father, in the hospital, 700 miles away in Toronto.

"Dear James," it began. "The doctors say I am making good progress, but the way things look I won't be home for close on a month. When I do get around I've

[3]

got to go slow all winter. It seems to be up to you and Lindsay.

"That trap-line down the Squaw we looked over last year ought to give you a good catch of fur. Lindsay could handle the Poplar Lake and Squaw Lake country I think. And Ida and Mary could make a few sets around Wababimiga till I get back. You'll want to be going in soon.

"Don't worry any about me. I'm not done yet by a long shot. Take care of things and see your Mother has plenty of wood. The grub will last till the buyer comes and we can sell some fur. Love to all, Your Father."

It was hard to think of that great, powerful frame lying helpless in a hospital bed. "Big Lindsay" Vanderbeck, six feet three in his socks, who could pack a hundred pounds of duffel and two hind-quarters of moose meat all day—who could pole a canoe up the stiffest rapids in Ontario, and break trail more hours on end than any white man north of the track.

Jim squared his shoulders. That letter had made him feel the load of his responsibility. His boyhood, it appeared, was over. Now, at eighteen, he had suddenly become the man of the family.

"Supper, boys," called Ida, from the kitchen.

She was three years Jim's senior—a strongly built girl, fresh faced, dark haired—almost as tall as Jim himself. Mary, the younger sister, fair like their mother, was already at the table.

[4]

"Did you feed the dogs, Lindsay?" she asked, helping herself to fried moose steak.

The boy gave her yellow curls a tweak. "Not yet," he said. "Stuff wasn't cool enough. Listen to old Bruno holler."

From the log kennels at the rear of the house came the deep, impatient bark of the big lead dog, supplemented by a chorus of yelps and whines from the rest of the pack.

Lindsay took one boiled potato from the heaping bowl.

"You'd better eat more'n that," said Jim grimly. "Last regular potatoes you'll get for eight months. I aim to start tomorrow morning."

"Soon as that?" his mother looked at him in mild surprise.

"Yes," he answered. "I saw some geese flying. If there's an early freeze, we won't have much time."

Mrs. Vanderbeck nodded imperturbably. "That's right," she said. "I'll go over those wool socks tonight. The rest of your clothes will do."

Supper over, the girls set about their dish washing, while Jim and Lindsay took a flashlight and went out to the kennels. A washboiler full of cooked corn meal and meat scraps stood cooling beside the embers of the outdoor fire. As they began ladling it into pans, all seven dogs set up a riot of hungry yelping and strained at their heavy chains.

[5]

They were of mixed breeds—two of them tall, rangy
police dogs, one or two pure huskies, and the rest a
cross of husky, Airedale and St. Bernard. All were big,
full furred and powerful—not racing dogs but strong,
steady pullers, built for hard work in the bush. They
would have torn a stranger to bits in a matter of minutes, but the boys clouted them out of the way with
impunity.

The leaders of the three teams were fed first, as
canine discipline demanded. Then the others, frantically waiting, got their pans of mush.

Jim looked them over critically. They were in good
condition. Soft, of course, from their summer in town,
but a few days of work in the snow would remedy
that.

"Another two weeks," he told Bruno, "and you'll be
eating whitefish again. It won't be long now."

Half an hour later the boys left their mother and
the girls darning a basketful of heavy gray socks and
went down the track to the storehouse. It was one of
the few frame buildings in town, the Vanderbecks'
place of business ever since they had come out to
Nakina in 1925. Here the cans and cases and bags of
food were stored—the tents and bed-rolls and pack-
sacks. Grub and outfits for the parties of hunters and
fishermen who journeyed up from the States and Eastern Canada each summer. They had followed Lindsay
Vanderbeck from his old haunts on the New Bruns-

wick salmon rivers, out to this vaster, wilder, more abundant country in the North. In steadily increasing numbers they had come, until two years before. Then, with the grip of the Depression tightening over the continent, guides and outfitters had found themselves almost without employment.

The Vanderbecks were more fortunate than some. They had among their patrons a few loyal sportsmen with enough wealth to go into the bush regardless of conditions. But even so, there had not been enough business the last two years to make a living.

Jim looked ruefully around the big half empty place, wondering whether he would ever see it filled again and busy. His own outfit and Lindsay's were stacked along one wall. With a notebook and pencil they went over the items one by one.

There were 200 pounds of flour, 50 pounds of sugar, 25 pounds of beans. There were half a dozen big cans of dried milk and as many of baking powder, and of jam. There were cartons of macaroni and several sacks of potatoes and boxes of dried fruit. There were tea, cocoa, salt, candles and matches, along with a few other woods necessities. In three big bags there were 300 pounds of corn meal for the dogs. Beside the piles of food stood their guns and eiderdowns, axes and paddles, and there were five or six traps from the mail-order house. For the most part they would use last year's traps, stored at their line camps in the bush.

Everything was there, Jim found, checking the list for the third time. They would be ready to start in the morning. Down at the station he found the owner of the town's one motor truck, and made arrangements to have their supplies hauled to the lake.

The Limited had come and gone, but a handful of Indians and white men still lolled in the lee of the red frame station building, out of the wind.

"Hi, Jim," they said, one after another. "Hi, Jim."

A short, compactly built French trapper climbed down off his perch on the baggage truck.

"So," he smiled, "you're goin' in, eh?"

Jim nodded. "Tomorrow. When are you startin', Emile?"

"Oh, pretty quick. I jus' come back from down in my country. Plenty rabbits, this year. That ought to make plenty fisher."

"See any moose?"

"Oh, sure. Two or three cows an' calves. Some young bulls. I see your party got a nice head. That's fine, Jim. You make a good guide. What do you hear from your dad?"

Jim told him such news as he had. "I guess Lindsay and I'll be trapping for the family this winter," he said with a certain pride.

Emile Coté grinned. "That's right," he said. "You boys'll catch plenty fur, I bet. You got a good country, Jim. That Squaw River country's full o' mink."

The Frenchman's face turned serious then, and he lowered his voice a little. "I come by your family's place on Waba, two-three days ago," he said. "Everything's all right. Only maybe they'll have some company this year. That Cree, Joe Leake, has come back. Got a camp 'bout three mile from you. Eskimo squaw an' six kids. They'll kill a lot o' moose, I expect. Set some traps, too."

"They'll be all right," said Jim. "There's room in that country. An' Ma gets along with 'em fine. Well, good luck, Emile! Hope you catch a lot o' fur. We'll be getting an early start in the morning."

He shook hands with his friend, picked up Lindsay at the station restaurant, and set out for home along the ties. The wind had died to a whisper and the cold was more intense. From behind them, down in the Indian settlement, came the faint, wailing howl of a husky dog. And off to the right, above the black spearpoints of the spruces, wavering fingers of white and blue and green went searching up the sky.

"Look at those Northern Lights," said Jim. "Change of weather, I reckon. Ought to be a cold, clear day tomorrow."

Lynx

II

THERE were only five miles of road in Nakina, and three of those miles ran past tiny clearings and rough log shacks to the shore of Cordingley Lake. Autumn rains and frost had made a quagmire of the dark clay. The truck, loaded with the boys' supplies, pulled slowly and laboriously through the mud. And twice they had to pry it out of holes where it was bogged to the rear axle.

When at last they reached the landing it was nearly noon. The driver helped them pile their outfits on a rocky ledge by the water, then turned his truck around and waved a friendly farewell. It would be weeks before they saw another human being.

The two eighteen-foot canoes were racked up in a

spruce thicket close to the landing. They brought Lindsay's down first and stowed it carefully, tying a tarpaulin over the bulky cargo. Then Jim's canoe was put into the water and loaded.

On that southern arm of the lake there was less than a mile of open water for the wind to sweep. Nevertheless the waves came in on the rocks with a sullen chop. There was a scud of clouds from the north and the lake looked cold and gray and forbidding.

"Pull that tarp good and tight," Jim warned. "We'll be bucking a wind when we get around the point."

They took their paddles and shoved off. The first two miles were comparatively easy, for they were able to cut across to the opposite shore and keep in the lee of the woods. Then they saw racing whitecaps coming past the point ahead, and in a few moments they swung their bows northeast, directly into the wind's teeth.

"Boy, oh, boy!" yelled Lindsay, "we're goin' to do some work on this stretch!"

"You better save your breath," retorted his older brother. "Keep her nose straight in, an' don't ship any more water 'n you have to."

They had to fight for every inch of the next five miles. When at last Jim brought his canoe abreast of the pointed rock, for which the lake had once been named, he was glad the battle was nearly over. With every pitch of the bow, white spray rattled over the tarpaulin, and he could see water sloshing around his boots in the bottom.

Lindsay was toiling along in his wake, his young face set hard, and his shoulders pumping to the quick, whiplike paddle stroke of the north woods. A good, game kid, thought Jim with pride.

The waves were lower now. They eased into the quiet water of Cranberry River, and rested tired backs and arms.

"I nearly swamped, back there," Lindsay panted. "We'd better haul out and see how much of our stuff got wet."

There was a grassy cove a hundred yards ahead, and they beached the canoes, unloading their cargoes. Nearly everything was wet around the edges but the only part of their supplies that was wholly spoiled was a hundred-pound sack of corn meal. Regretfully, they dumped it, drained the canoes and started packing once more.

Jim straightened up suddenly. "Listen!" he whispered. "Ducks!" There was a croaking quack high above them and a pair of belated mallards nosed down into the wind for a landing.

Right under Lindsay's hand was Jim's new 12-gauge shotgun, loaded. The younger boy had it at his shoulder in a jiffy, and as he fired, the drake came tumbling down in shoal water, not twenty yards away. Then the second barrel roared and the duck dropped like a plummet.

[12]

"Got 'em both," the youngster cried exultantly. "How about dinner right here?"

"No," said Jim. "You had a big breakfast. Let's push along. I guess you'll admit that's a pretty good gun, though?"

"It'll do," Lindsay replied, rubbing his shoulder, "even if it does kick like a mule. O' course, there's a lot in who handles it."

Jim grinned. "Yep," he said, "there's nothing wrong with your shooting."

They loaded the canoes, picked up the floating ducks, and resumed their journey. For four miles, the little river twisted like a snake through the bush. There were two short portages, and it took time to transport the duffel across. With tump-lines—the leather straps that go across the forehead and tie under the load— they could each pack 150 pounds at a time, but it was necessary to make three trips at each carry. First the sacks of flour and meal and the grub boxes. Then the heavy duffel, with the sleeping-bags and other bulky things piled high on top. And finally, the shoulder packs and canoes. To pick up an 18-foot canoe when you are already loaded with a 60-pound pack-sack, is no easy feat. But to these youngsters, woods trained almost since their birth, portaging was as natural as walking. Their muscles moved instinctively in the easy leverage that lifts a canoe and swings it into place on the shoulders like the shell of a giant beetle.

It was four o'clock when they paddled out of the river mouth into Poplar Lake. The wind had died down and they were able to go at better speed. "Come on," called Jim over his shoulder, "we want to make camp before dark. Only three miles more!"

There was a cabin on the north shore of the lake, built by Jim and his father the year before. It was snug enough, with a small stove, a hand-hewn table and bench, and a pole bed built into one corner.

They made camp methodically but quickly. While Lindsay cleaned the ducks, Jim felled a dry jack-pine and split a good-sized pile of firewood. Then, as the meat sizzled over the fire, they unloaded the canoes, brought the perishable goods inside, and spread a tarpaulin over the rest. This was to be Lindsay's home camp for the winter, so most of his outfit would be left here.

Biscuits, baked by Mrs. Vanderbeck that morning, and a pot of hot cocoa supplemented the rich, dark meat of the mallards. The boys ate till they could hold no more, then piled the bed with fresh balsam boughs and climbed into their eiderdowns. Outside, the wind went sighing through the spruce tops, and the water lapped softly in the reeds. In two minutes they were sound asleep.

* * * *

TRAP-LINES NORTH

At six o'clock Jim woke to a noise of hammering. Lindsay, already dressed, was tacking something up on the wall.

"It's a calendar," he explained. "I remembered how we had to tally the days on a stick last year, and I brought it from home. Let's see, yesterday was October tenth, wasn't it? And today's the eleventh. Only three weeks before the trapping season opens. Think we can have everything ready?"

"Not this way," answered Jim, and bounded out of bed. "Brrr! Let's get that fire going."

It was a quick job. The dry, resinous splints of pine, feathered into plumes of shavings by Lindsay's big jackknife, caught at the first flare of the match. In five minutes the little stove was filling the cabin with welcome warmth.

While Jim cooked flapjacks, his brother separated his share of the winter supplies and stowed them away in the camp. Then they breakfasted, loaded the canoes and made a start.

The wind had died in the night and the air was clear, with a sharp tang of frost. They paddled down Poplar Lake, made a half-mile carry into Grave Lake and traversed its four miles of open water. An hour's paddling through the bends and reaches of another small river brought them to the head of Squaw Lake. They picked a likely camping place where the shore

[15]

rose steeply from the lake, and beached the canoes. With their two axes ringing steadily in the bush, it took only a short time to throw up a half wall, four logs high, on which to pitch their small tent. This done they set about one of the most important of the fall chores—netting fish.

Jim had run nets at the inlet of Squaw Lake before and knew just where the fish would be thickest. Each end of the long gill net was fastened, top and bottom, to a spruce pole, which the boys drove down as firmly as possible into the mud. The net had a mesh about two and a half inches square—just large enough to hold the head of an average sized fish.

They went back to their new camp for lunch and it was two hours later when they returned to tend the net. Both were in one canoe, Jim steering, Lindsay in the bow. As they rounded a wooded point the younger boy suddenly stopped paddling and reached stealthily behind him. Jim followed the direction of his eyes. There on the bank, not a hundred yards away, stood a big buck deer, perfectly still, watching them with no sign of alarm.

"Aw, thunder!" muttered Lindsay, looking foolish. "I was all set to grab the rifle. Forgot we'd left it in the tent. And what a shot!"

Jim laughed. "Maybe we'll have time to go back for it. He doesn't seem to be in any hurry."

But even as he spoke, the deer turned with a leisurely

movement, flirted his white tail at them, and ambled into the bush.

There were fish in the net. They could see the poles shake as they paddled nearer. Starting at one end, they pulled in the coarse mesh hand over hand, and soon had twenty good-sized whitefish, bullheads and suckers floundering in the bottom of the canoe.

Back at camp, they were busy until nearly supper time cleaning their catch. Then a hole was cut in the tail of each fish, a stick run through, and they were hung on a high rack, out of the reach of four-footed marauders.

It was dark when they started the fire and they took their time over an excellent supper. Jim had found a comfortable bed of moss to sit on and leaned back with his shoulders against a tree, luxuriously sipping the last of his cocoa.

"Oh, boy," he murmured. "This is what I call—"

But he never got out the last word, for at that instant there was an ear-splitting scream in the woods right behind him.

"Good gosh!" whispered Lindsay shakily. "Wh— what do you s'pose that was?"

Both boys stumbled to their feet. "Lynx, I guess," Jim answered. "Sounded like somebody bein' murdered, didn't it? Get the flashlight. I'll take the rifle."

They were glad to stay close together as they moved cautiously into the woods. A little way back of the tent the ground pitched downward into a swamp, filled with evergreen thickets and a snarl of fallen trees.

"I can't see him, can you?" asked Lindsay, his teeth chattering.

"Don't shake that light so," Jim whispered. "Hold it steady. Maybe we'll flash his eyes."

But the beam of the torch fell on nothing but tangled brush and dark, mucky pools. The scream was not repeated, and after a few minutes both youngsters were glad to come back to the cheery glow of the fire.

It was comforting to feel the solid thickness of the log wall between them and the night when they turned in. They lay there, snug in their eiderdowns, and discussed the noise they had heard.

"I'm certain now, it must have been a lynx," Jim argued. "I've heard Emile tell about hearing 'em—just like a woman hollering. Come to think of it, he said it was the smell of fresh fish around the camp that brought 'em. Just like any cat. Maybe I'd better see if those fish of ours are safe."

He crawled out of the sleeping-bag and went to the tent door. The fire had been quenched before they left it, and there was no light but the pale glimmer from the lake. Jim turned the flash in the direction of the fish rack and pressed the switch. Something went crashing off through the brush—a good-sized animal, by the noise it made.

"Get out o' there!" yelled the boy loudly, and threw

a chunk of wood after the intruder. The fish on the rack were undisturbed, he found, and when he had made sure they were hung at a safe height, he returned to bed.

The boys rose early, to another fair day. As soon as breakfast was finished, they prepared to pull the net again.

"Hold on," said Jim, as Lindsay was launching the canoe. "This time we want that rifle along."

He went into the tent for it and his younger brother heard sounds of wrath as he emerged.

"Darn! Look at that!" Jim cried. "The front sight's gone, I must have hit it on a tree in that fool hunt of ours last night!"

For five minutes they searched the rough ground back of the camp, but the bit of metal was thoroughly lost.

"What could we make one of?" Lindsay asked. "I know—have you got any money—a penny or something?"

Delving in his pockets Jim finally produced a nickel. Laying it edgewise against the slot in the rifle barrel, he gave a whistle of surprise. "It'll fit!" he exclaimed. "You do have good ideas sometimes, kid!"

Jim went to his "possible" sack, the small canvas bag that held his personal necessities—and took out a file, and when the edges of the coin had been chopped off, he worked the metal down to something like the right size. A little careful hammering drove it home firmly in the slot. Jim sighted along the barrel and shook his head dubiously.

"Doesn't look bad," Lindsay ventured.

"I don't know," the older boy replied. "I expect these things have to be made just so—accurate to the thousandth of an inch. Old Man Winchester would probably throw a fit if he saw it. Well, it'll have to do. Let's get started."

The new sight was given a test before it was ten minutes old. They came around the point, half hoping to see yesterday's buck. Instead there was a big, dark animal, knee deep in the grass at the water's edge—a young bull moose!

"Hold her as she is," breathed Jim. He laid down his paddle and picked up the .32. As he cocked it and brought the stock to his shoulder the moose lifted its head, looking toward them. The distance was about 200 yards. Jim notched the shining bead of nickel squarely in the rear sight and laid it on the big beast's head as he pressed the trigger.

The moose staggered, hit hard, and at the next shot down he went.

Paddling breathlessly toward the spot, Jim waited, half expecting to see his quarry rise and scamper off. But the brown bulk in the grass did not move.

"Look at that!" cried Lindsay. "Right between the

eyes! Who says there's anything wrong with that front sight?"

They pulled the moose a few yards to dry ground and began skinning operations. Neither of the boys was a greenhorn at this job. They had done it many times before, and the young bull's hide peeled smartly off the firm flesh. When the carcass was laid bare, Jim cut it into quarters and they loaded the canoe.

The next few hours were spent back at the tent, building a special rack for the meat and stretching the hide over a log. Later on, the hair would be scraped off and the hide cut into strips for snowshoe filling.

"There," said Jim, when they had finished. "Enough meat to last till Christmas, looks like. How about a nice pan of fresh moose liver for dinner. Must be 'most time to eat."

They fried part of the liver and enjoyed a repast that any epicure might envy. Then they visited the net once more, and took out between thirty and forty fish. Before they had done cleaning them the afternoon was almost gone.

"Well, we can start traveling in the morning with a clear conscience," Jim yawned. "Got all the fish we need for a while, and a good supply of meat that we can pick up on the way back. Come—get to work, young feller—it's your turn to cook supper!"

Musk Rat

III

SQUAW LAKE is more than ten miles in length, but nowhere much over a mile and a half wide. It meanders through the bush like an overgrown river, its shores cut deeply by innumerable bays and coves.

On a point nearly half way down the lake, the two young Vanderbecks landed, that morning of the 13th of October. Jim led the way up from the water.

"If you've never seen it," he told Lindsay, "it's worth a look. We ought to stop and pay our respects any way. Most of the trappers do, when they pass this way."

After a moment they came to a little cleared space, and in the middle of it a low mound of earth, with a wooden cross set up at one end. Hanging on the cross was a big old nickel-plated watch.

"Here's where he's buried," the older brother explained. "An Indian boy—died here about twelve years ago. He was prouder of that watch than anything he owned, so they hung it on the grave. It's been out here in the cold an' snow for twelve winters an' still runs!"

He saw disbelief on Lindsay's face and laughed. "No, no," he said, "I don't mean it keeps running all the time. But if you wind it, it'll go."

They stepped nearer, careful not to tread on the grave, and Jim wound and set the weather-beaten timepiece.

"Now listen," he suggested.

Lindsay put his ear closer to the watch. Sure enough he could hear its labored ticking and see the rusty hands begin to move.

"Sa-a-ay!" he breathed, in a tone of awe, "that *is* some watch! It's a wonder somebody hasn't stolen it."

"Off a grave?" Jim countered. "No Indian would. And the white men are scared he'd haunt 'em."

A few miles farther on, the boys came to a cove where a narrow little river emptied into the lake. Jim, in the forward canoe, pushed into the mouth of the stream and waited for Lindsay to come alongside.

"This is the outlet from Sucker Lake," he said. "The camp isn't far—two or three miles and no carries. Keep in the same channel I do, and watch for snags."

Paddling cautiously in the shoal water, they came

out after a while on a fair-sized lake.

"Camp's right over there," called Jim. "You can't see it through the trees, but the landing's close to that big rock."

They beached the canoes and came in sight of a small log cabin among the spruces.

"Huh!" said Lindsay. "I thought you said it was new and weather-tight. Look at that roof!"

Jim, who had been walking up the trail, paused in consternation. "What in thunder—" he exclaimed. "Why, it *was* new. I nailed that tar paper on myself. Looks as if a tornado struck it."

On the side nearest them, more than half the heavy roofing paper was torn away. It hung in long shreds from the eaves, leaving the bare poles exposed. They hurried to the cabin and unlatched the door, but inside nothing appeared to be disturbed. Stove, grub box, table and bed were just as Jim remembered leaving them.

Outdoors once more, they made a closer inspection of the wrecked roof. "I know!" cried Lindsay. "It was a bear. Look at those claw marks—the old son-of-a-gun!"

In the bark of a jack-pine that stood close to the eaves there were deep scratches. And still more and deeper ones showed on the stout poles of the roof.

"He sure wanted to get in," Jim frowned. "What do you s'pose he was after? Oh—I remember now. We left

a chunk of bacon in the grub box! Thought I smelled
something rancid when we were inside. Well, we'll just
have to do some sort of a patching job."

They cut a good-sized tree and peeled the bark as
best they could with their axes, laying the uneven strips
in overlapping layers on the poles. To hold them down
they brought stones from the lake. Then they went
inside.

Jim looked upward and saw large chinks of daylight
still shining through. "Well, Lindsay," he laughed,
"she'll be tight enough with about a foot o' snow on
top. You'll have to keep an awful small fire though, or
you'll melt your roof!"

"Yeah," the younger brother growled. "Old bear
would have to do it to one o' my camps. All for your
rotten bacon, too."

They cleaned out the grub box and deposited a few
of the provisions. That was the purpose of this trip—
to leave supplies at each of the line-camps. The afternoon was well along when they had the place shipshape, and there was no use in going farther that night.

"What say we take the shotgun and see if we can
find some more ducks?" Lindsay suggested.

They got into one of the canoes and paddled quietly
along the shore of Sucker Lake. At each marshy cove
they looked hopefully for ducks but there was neither
sign nor sound of them.

The boys were just about to turn homeward, when

they heard the plaintive bawl of a cow moose ahead.

"Come on—let's see if we can see her," Jim whispered.

Paddling stealthily, they worked the canoe around the next point. A large cow and her calf were feeding in the marsh grass, two or three hundred yards up the lake. Again the moose lifted her head and sent the sound echoing from shore to shore. Almost at once a deeper bellow answered her—a roaring call that sounded so close the boys jumped.

Then right in front of them, a bare half dozen canoe lengths from where they sat, a giant black bull came out of the woods.

"Boy, what a head!" whispered Lindsay. The big moose turned at the sound and looked directly at them.

His antlers had a magnificent spread—sixty inches, Jim estimated afterward—and he looked seven or eight feet tall, where he stood at the water's edge.

"Let's get out where we can see better," Jim murmured, and the canoe moved quietly toward the middle of the lake. The cow and calf had winded them now, and started leisurely for the higher ground. Until they had vanished into the bush, the bull did not move. He was standing guard. At length he gave a scornful snort and wheeled about. He passed into the dark of the trees as silently as he had come.

Jim sighed. "Too bad to miss a shot like that," he said, "but he had too fine a head to kill for meat. I sure wish we'd had a hunting party along! Still, maybe he'll be here next fall."

The sun had set behind a bank of cold looking clouds when they reached the cabin.

"Wind's in the southwest," Jim remarked, sniffing the frosty air. "Feels like a change in the weather. We'd better get to bed early and make my home camp if we can before a storm gets here."

His prophecy proved accurate, for the next morning was bleak and overcast. They shut up the camp and took the two canoes down the outlet brook to Squaw Lake. As the shores narrowed and the current hurried them into the head of Squaw River, the first flurries of snow began to drive across the water.

"Steady, now!" yelled Jim. "River's high and those rapids'll be fast. Better get your pole handy."

In five minutes it was snowing heavily, blurring their vision as they bent forward, trying to gauge the current ahead. The first few rapids they shot with the paddle, running down fast through the white water. But there were worse places below.

Jim saw a treacherous part of the channel leaping nearer through the driving snow, and stood up, balancing the setting pole. Lindsay, behind him, followed suit. They had been down the Squaw many times before, and each of its perils was familiar to them. But veiled by the snow the landmarks were hard to recognize. Twice Jim's pole slipped on smooth rock before he found the hold he sought. Finally he was able to check his speed and ease the canoe down, past hungry rocks and swirling eddies.

There was smoother water below, and he looked around to see Lindsay—as good a canoeman as himself —paddling close alongside. The younger boy grinned. "Take any water?"

"Only a drop or two. How about you?"

"Dry as a bone!"

The cabin that was to be Jim's home camp for the winter was seven miles down the river. It took them less than an hour to reach it, thanks to the high water. But when they hauled out on the shore beside the cabin it was snowing too hard to make further progress possible that day. They unloaded the canoes and carried the supplies indoors.

This camp was much like the others they had visited. A French trapper had built it some years before and sold it to the Vanderbecks. The log walls enclosed a room about twelve feet square. The stove, in its box of sand, filled one corner, and the pole bed another. There was a table made of puncheons—broad, split logs—and a rude chair of hand-hewn wood. The floor was beaten earth. In each side wall there was a small square window, with overlapping panes of glass.

"Pretty slick, isn't it?" asked Jim, casting an appreciative eye around the place.

"It'll do," said Lindsay. "At least it's got a roof. But

I'm cold—let's get that stovepipe up!"

They fitted the rusty pipe into place at the back of the tin stove, and Jim scrambled to the roof to remove the flat rock that had covered the hole. A whisky-jack flapped through the spruce boughs overhead and cursed him volubly, ruffling dark feathers against the snow.

"Some welcome!" the boy grinned. "Get out o' here, you robber!" And he shied a chip with vindictive aim at the big gray bird.

Canada jays, commonly known as whisky-jacks, or gorbies, were old enemies of his. They were always to be found around a camp—bold, saucy, thieving fellows —the clowns of the North Woods.

With the stovepipe ready, the boys took their axes and went after a supply of wood. There was plenty of dry jack-pine and spruce within a short distance of the camp, and in three minutes they had each felled a tree. Then, shouldering the long butt logs, they returned to the little cleared space beside the cabin. With both axes ringing steadily there was soon a neat pile of firewood by the door and a cheerful thread of smoke eddying from the chimney.

"You stay here," Jim told his brother. "Keep her going and get the place warmed up. I'll start out for some bedding. If I'm going to live here, I'd better get the lay of the land."

He set out, whistling, his ax on his shoulder. The force of the storm was lessened by the thick woods, but wind-driven particles of snow sifted down constantly around his head, and in the swaying tops, far above, there was a sound like the moan and beat of the sea.

Ranging through the bush for nearly half a mile, he finally found what he wanted. It was a clump of balsams huddled close together as if for comfort in the blast. He cut a small tree and was starting to drag it back with him when he caught sight of a round ball of gray-brown feathers on a limb just over his head. It was a birch partridge—the silliest and most helpless of all birds in the North Woods. He could have reached it with a stick as it sat there watching him with a foolish eye. However, the Canadian game laws wisely protect birch partridges. That is to give an unarmed man, lost in the bush, some assurance of finding fresh meat.

The gray twilight of the storm and the whirling snow would have confused a tenderfoot's sense of direction. But Jim had unconsciously memorized every rock and fallen tree he had passed. Without actually thinking about it, he followed his back track unerringly.

When he reached the cabin he trimmed off the soft, springy boughs of fir, and carried in a great armful to lay over the pole floor of the bed.

"You've got a couple of holes here that need chinking," Lindsay remarked. "Feel that draft?"

There was a crack between the logs where a tiny pile

of snow had sifted through.

"Hm," said Jim. "Seems to me I remember a good patch of moss, back there along the river." He went out again and soon returned with enough of the spongy gray-green stuff to pack the crevices inside and out.

Lindsay had started cooking their noon meal, and when it was eaten they had the prospect of an afternoon indoors. At the back of the cabin there was a big box, built of logs with a sloping tar-papered lid to keep out the rain. In it was a pile of traps, left there by their father after the spring muskrat trapping.

The boys carried them inside by armfuls and spent several hours cleaning and sorting them. There were all sizes from No. 1 and 1½ jump-traps to big No. 4's that would hold a lynx or a coyote. Some needed minor repairs, which could be made with the ordinary tools they had with them. A few were damaged beyond fixing.

There was still an hour of daylight when the snow stopped falling. Lindsay took a look around outside and reported several inches on the ground and a cold wind blowing. Jim, meanwhile, had taken a little black notebook and the stub of a pencil out of his possible-sack, and was writing up his diary for the past five days.

They ate an early supper and made everything ready for a quick start in the morning. With winter shutting down they would have little time to spare, these next

[31]

few days.

The chill of dawn found them already dressed and eating breakfast, while the dry pine crackled merrily in the stove. They left one of the canoes here, and loaded the other with the tent, bed-rolls, traps and a few provisions to be distributed among Jim's line-camps.

They paddled slowly down the Squaw, stopping at frequent intervals to fix up "cubbies" along the shore. Most of these cubbies, or trap-houses, had been built a year or more before. They resembled tiny lean-tos, two or three feet high, laid up against a tree. A couple of sloping sticks, nailed or braced to the sides of the tree, supported a rough shelter of boughs, and under it a notched log was slanted from the ground to the tree trunk. Some of the cubbies had wings built out on either side, to keep an animal from reaching the bait except by way of the trap.

It was nearly evening when they reached the head of the Long Portage. The gray sky was beginning to spit snow once more.

Jim chose a No. 2 trap to lay beside a cubby he had just finished repairing, and straightened up.

"How do you want to go?" he asked. "It's a long haul by land—two miles and rough footing. By the river it's six, but we can get through in a few minutes if we get through at all. With this high water we might make out all right over those rocks."

Lindsay looked at the portage trail, then back at the rapids. The river below ran like a wild horse, tossing its white mane. "I'll vote for the river," he grinned.

"All right," Jim nodded. "But remember, it won't be any picnic."

They got in, bow and stern, and Jim pushed off. A cautious stroke or two took them into the middle of the current. The drive of the water was strong here, and the channel deep—too deep for setting poles. It had to be run with the paddle. They swept down dizzily with white waves lifting above the gunwales.

"Rock!" yelled Lindsay, pointing to the left, and Jim swung the bobbing craft out with a quick turn of the wrist. There was calmer water below, and a bend in the river, where they both paddled hard to keep out of the eddies. Then came more rapids, each one rougher and swifter than the last.

"Only one more to shoot!" Jim cried encouragingly. They were entering the head of a long, twisting slant of water and the roar of it was already in their ears. The canoe leaped like a crazy thing in the tumbling crests. Once they slithered around a big black rock with only inches to spare. Once they were spun end-for-end in the whirlpool at a bend, but the light craft straightened out in answer to a few quick strokes of the paddle.

Jim drew a deep, exultant breath. They were almost through! At that very instant there was a cry of dismay from Lindsay, and their speed was checked so suddenly that Jim sprawled forward on top of the duffel bags. The canoe tilted far to one side. It was caught squarely across a big log.

"Stay where you are," called Jim. He stepped out on the log, grasping the gunwale. But before he could lift the canoe against the weight of water that was already filling it, his foot skidded from under him. The next second he was in the icy rapids up to his chest.

"I'm all right," he told Lindsay through chattering teeth. "Get ready now—I'm going to pull her off!"

A powerful heave succeeded in sliding the craft off the log and he pushed it ahead of him into quieter water before scrambling ashore. Lindsay landed fifty yards farther down and was hauling out the drenched cargo when Jim arrived.

"G-g-gimme an ax—quick!" the older boy shivered. A dead spruce, with gray "squaw's whiskers" trailing from its branches, stood close to the bank. Jim braced his numb legs and swung his ax with a vicious bite. A dozen such blows and the tree came down. Lindsay had gathered a pile of dry twigs and was nursing the flame of a match. It caught. By the time Jim could get there with an armful of split kindling they had a fire. And stick by stick they built it into a roaring blaze.

"Golly," Jim murmured, as he toasted the seat of his breeches, "I sure am grateful to the old chap that invented fire!"

Otter

IV

WHEN Jim's clothing had dried out, the boys set up the tent and looked over the canoe and its cargo to see what damage had been done. Most of the paint was scraped off the bottom of the canoe but fortunately there was no tear in the canvas. Only a little of the food was spoiled, and the waterproof coverings of the sleeping-bags had kept them dry inside.

"We were pretty lucky, at that," said Lindsay, as they ate supper. "Next time, I'll think twice before I turn down a nice, comfortable, two-mile carry."

"We wouldn't have been so lucky, if you hadn't kept those matches dry," Jim answered. "I've broken trail at fifty below, and didn't feel half as chilly as I did before we got that fire going."

It must have been ten or twelve degrees under the freezing mark that night, and though the snow had ceased at dark, a boisterous wind still wailed in the spruces. The tent, solidly pegged down, gave them some shelter from the cold. Once they were inside the eiderdown sleeping-bags a drowsy warmth came over them. The wind in the trees was a soothing sound that soon lulled them to sleep.

When dawn came, the weather had cleared again. They went over the canoe inch by inch, patching the worst scrapes with black tar. Then they reloaded and set out down the Squaw. There was only one rapid of any consequence in the eight-mile stretch to Beaver Lake Portage. They shot it without mishap, and hauled out at the head of the carry about two in the afternoon.

One trip across the mile-and-a-half trail was all they needed to pack supplies to a lean-to cabin on Beaver Lake. They returned in time to pitch their tent and make camp near the portage landing.

Next morning they continued their cruise down the Squaw, patching up cubbies and leaving traps as they went. Jim's last camp was seven or eight miles lower— a good thirty-five miles from Lindsay's winter quarters at the foot of Squaw Lake. They found the cabin in bad shape, part of one wall tumbled in and the roof sagging. To rebuild it took the best part of the next two days—October 19 and 20.

The weather held clear and cold. The afternoon of the 20th they went down along the river shore to fix up an outlying trap-line. Coming out of a chute of white water they slid into a broad pool as quiet as a mill pond. And along the farther bank, Lindsay sighted an arrowlike ripple. "Look!" he warned. "Something swimming!"

Jim saw it, too—a round, sleek head that looked like a dog's, and a long, streamlined body cutting the water.

"Otter!" he said. "A nice skin. Why weren't you born part Indian, Lindsay?"

No white man is allowed to kill beaver and otter in Ontario. Those two valuable furs are reserved as part of the immemorial heritage of the Indian hunter.

The two boys sat statue-still in the canoe and let it drift silently closer. If the otter saw them it showed no sign of fear. Out from a clump of dry grass swam a second animal—its mate perhaps—and the pair cruised along in company for fifty yards or more. Then Lindsay struck the water a resounding slap with his paddle and in a twinkling the otters had dived out of sight.

Twenty minutes later, working together on a trap-house a few feet from the river bank, they caught a glimpse of another fur-bearer. Right under their noses the sinuous, dark body of a mink glided out of a thicket and made for the water.

Jim looked after him gloatingly. "I'll be seeing you again, big feller!" he exclaimed. "I know just the spot to catch you in a water-set."

Lindsay pretended to be envious. "Look at all the fur there is down here!" he snorted. "Anybody could be a trapper with mink runnin' right over his feet."

Jim grinned, then turned serious. "It's a funny thing, though. Did you notice we haven't seen or heard a moose since we left your ground? I've been wonderin' about that. There hasn't even been a track this side o' Sucker Lake."

"Yep, it's queer, all right," the younger brother nodded. "Dad always called this good moose country, down the Squaw."

They were nearly at the end of the trap-line now. A short paddle took them across a broad, shallow place in the river and they stopped a few minutes to watch the trout spawning on the sandbars—huge, gleaming fish, with spots of blue and scarlet enameled on their silver sides.

"I'd like to show this to some of our fishing parties from the States," Jim laughed. "Would their eyes pop out? Look at that old walloper—seven pounds if he's an ounce!"

At the entrance of a little brook, on the south side of the river, they landed to set up a cubby. Jim could find no pole to his liking near the spot, and taking the ax he went a short distance up the brook, looking for a dead spruce. The snow, three or four inches deep, was ideal for tracking. He had gone only a few yards when he stopped with a whoop of joy. There was the unmistakable trail of a fisher crossing toward the bank of the little stream.

"What is it?" called Lindsay.

"Fisher track," he answered. "Here's some mink sign, too. And say—I'll take it all back about the moose! A young bull or a cow left here in a hurry a little while ago."

"Let's see," said Lindsay, plowing through the underbrush. They bent together over the fresh, deep prints, then looked ahead to see where the moose had gone.

"No use trailing, I reckon," said Jim. "I left the rifle at camp, and I think it's a cow, anyway."

Lindsay did not answer for a moment. He had gone on a little way into the woods. When his voice came it had a note of amazement in it.

"Good—gosh!" Jim heard him say, and went to join his brother at a run. Alongside the moose track was an entirely different mark in the snow. A great, oval-shaped print with the plain impressions of four toe-pugs. It looked like a dog track but it was bigger—so big that the boys rubbed their eyes and peered again.

"Do you believe," said Jim in an awe-stricken voice, "that any wolf ever lived big enough to make that track?"

"Search me," Lindsay answered. "Look at this!" He pulled off his mitten and laid his flattened hand squarely in the footprint.

"Just a fit!" he murmured grimly. "Must be more'n seven inches long. No, of course I don't believe it—but

[39]

there it is!"

That was the last clear track of the wolf's paw. From that point on he was running in tremendous leaps that scattered the snow and left only blurred depressions.

"Come on," Jim urged, "let's see if he caught the moose!"

The chase was easy to follow, for the frightened quarry had crashed a two-foot path straight through the woods. Once the trail was trampled for several feet in all directions, and there was a broad furry hollow in the snow at one side.

"Moose stopped an' tried to fight," Jim translated the sign. "Wolf rolled out o' the way of her forefeet an' jumped over this way. She took a couple more jabs at him an' then started runnin' again. Watch out now!"

They followed on, and after a scant dozen strides Lindsay pointed silently ahead. There was a little open space where the snow was red and trodden. In the middle of it lay the carcass of a young cow moose.

"Wait," Jim cautioned. "Look around and see if there are any other wolf tracks. If he did this job alone it's the first time I ever heard of such a thing!"

They worked carefully around the patch of trampled snow where the death struggle had taken place. At the far edge of the clearing they found the single trail of the giant wolf angling off into the thick bush.

"All alone!" breathed Jim. "Boy—he must be a brute!"

Returning to the slain moose, they found both hind legs cleanly hamstrung and her throat laid open in a fearful gaping rent. The hide had also been torn at the loins and a good-sized chunk of meat ripped out.

"Well," Jim remarked, pulling out his knife, "there's no law against eating cow moose when somebody else kills it for you." And he laid back the skin and cut away the haunches.

Each of the boys picked up one of the pieces of meat. As they started back toward the half-finished cubby, Lindsay cast an uneasy glance behind him. "If that big devil is watching us," he said, "I'll feel a lot more comfortable when we get back to the rifle."

They reached camp just as darkness fell. A fire was soon crackling in the stove and Jim cut juicy slabs of moose steak to broil over the coals. That was a feast they remembered a long time. Not only was it delicious in every detail, but it marked the end of their exploring together. Tomorrow they would be starting back to their home camps, soon to separate for the winter.

Jim lay awake longer than usual that night. He was trying to remember something Joe Lagarde had told him once. Something about an enormous timber wolf down north on the Albany. He had given the story scant attention at the time, but he remembered how the Ojibway had muttered the dread name *"loup-garou."*

A *loup-garou*, Jim knew, was a sort of witch-wolf that could change at will from animal to human form. Queer how the Indians had picked up these old French superstitions along with their names. There was no word like that in Ojibway. A wolf was a wolf. You killed him on sight because he was a thief and a destroyer of game—also because there was a bounty on his gray hide. But as for being *afraid* of a wolf, you might as well go about in fear of a snowshoe rabbit!

He rolled over comfortably. A soft snore from the other eiderdown announced that Lindsay was already asleep. The wind had gone down and it was getting colder. Ice on the river in the morning. Ho, hum! His drowsy yawn was checked midway by a sudden sound in the bush—a deep-throated, quavering howl that rocketed high among the spruces and died away in gasping silence.

The boy sat bolt upright. A shiver ran down his spine and he could feel the short hair bristling at the back of his neck. Lindsay stirred and muttered but did not wake.

It seemed to take Jim a desperate while to pull on his breeches and boots. His hands fumbled at the laces, and his nerves were taut, waiting for a repetition of the wolf cry. At last he was ready. He groped for the rifle, threw off the safety catch and pushed open the door of the cabin. Outside, the snow and the bright starlight brought every detail of the camp into sharp relief. Not even the snap of a twig broke the stillness.

Jim stood there listening and watching for what must have been a full minute. Then he stepped softly over to the rack where they had slung the moose meat. The two hams were suspended from a pole, six or seven feet off the ground. Setting his rifle against a tree, the boy selected a higher crotch in which to brace the pole, and fastened it there securely. Reaching upward as far as his arm would stretch, his fingers missed the haunches of meat by more than a foot.

He waited several minutes longer, till the cold began to pierce his mackinaw, but the howl of the wolf did not come again. At last he went inside and undressed once more. When he returned to the warm sleeping-bag he felt a trifle ashamed. "Guess I was only half awake, and it scared me," he told himself. "Those Indian yarns give you fool notions." In no time at all he fell asleep.

＊　　＊　　＊　　＊

Lindsay's voice, loud and angry, broke into his morning dreams.

"The dirty, black-hearted so-and-so!" the youngster was raving. "I'll kill that big robber if I have to follow him all winter!"

Jim crawled hastily over the fir boughs to the door

[43]

of the hut.

"What's up?" he asked, but his eyes told him before the other boy could reply. The pole had been jerked down out of its crotch, and both haunches of moose meat were gone.

"Look!" cried Lindsay, pointing to a blur of tracks in the snow. "The same wolf—the big one! Why in thunder didn't we hang that meat out of reach?"

"I did," answered Jim in astonishment. "I heard him howl last night and came out and raised the pole. I swear it was ten feet high!"

Dressing quickly, he ran out to join his brother. "Here's the way I had it," he said, demonstrating with the long stick of spruce. "The meat was way up there, an' I had this end braced so strong it would bear a man's weight."

"Yeah?" said Lindsay, with ill-concealed doubt. "Maybe you dreamed it. Anyway the steaks are gone an' we'll have to go back to bacon for breakfast."

Jim bent over the tracks in the snow, then looked up, measuring the distance. "He jumped from here," he said, in a voice filled with awe. "Hit it from the side an' hung on. But to pull that pole loose he must weigh as much as I do—a hundred an' seventy or eighty pounds—gosh all hemlock! What a wolf!"

Lindsay began to be convinced. "If he's as big as that," he said, "he'd be worth going quite a ways to see. Boy, wouldn't his hide make a swell rug for the

cabin at Wababimiga? What say we go after him? Nobody can steal a week's grub from me an' get away
with it!"

Jim chuckled. "Maybe he felt the same way," he
suggested. "After all, it was his moose. No, kid, we're
not starting on any wolf hunt today. See that ice on
the river? That means we've got to hustle to get back."

There was no dodging this argument. A skim of ice
two or three feet wide extended out from the shore to
the edge of the current. If the cold continued they
would soon be unable to use the canoes. Stowing the
remains of their food and the duffel between the
thwarts, they launched their craft and made an early
start.

Beaver

V

THAT was a day of hard, unremitting work. They had
set Jim's home camp, 28 miles to the southwest, as their
goal, and there was no dawdling along the way. Where
the water was quiet enough for paddling, they paddled
steadily. When they came to rapids, they poled up
them, unless the current was too strong. In that case
they carried around. The light snow on the portages
was patterned with tracks—the clear, deep prints of
fisher—the narrow trough scooped by a mink's slim
body—and everywhere the delicate tracery left by
ermine, the little white weasels of the North.

There was still a greater head of water in the river
than they had expected, and some of the rapids they

JIM VANDERBECK. THE MOOSE ANTLERS ARE A PAIR PICKED UP IN
THE WOODS NEAR WABA

WINTER MEAT. MOOSE HAMS HUNG UP AFTER
skinning

BROWNIE, ONE OF THE LITTER OF PUPS BORN

MOOSE IN THE RIVER ABOVE THE LONG CARRY. JUNE, 1935

WHITE WATER ON THE LOWER SQUAW RIVER

YOUNG LINDSAY IN SUMMER COSTUME

THE FAMILY CABIN AT WABA. JIM SITTING ON THE FRONT PLATFORM

ONE OF JIM'S CAMPS ON SQUAW RIVER, MID-WINTER

IDA WITH SOME OF THE FAMILY'S SNOWSHOES

A PORCUPINE PAYS A VISIT TO CAMP

EMILE COTE AND HIS FAMOUS TEAM OF

BRUNO AND PAT, RESTING IN HARNESS

JOE AND MICHEL LAGARDE, INDIAN GUIDES

MIRANDA, THE PET FISHER, CLIMBS THE SIDE
OF HER CAGE FOR A BIT OF FOOD

"BIG LINDSAY" VANDERBECK

LINDSAY WITH SHORT FALL SNOWSHOES AND
SEVEN-FOOT WINTER SNOWSHOES

NETTING FISH THROUGH THE ICE. LINDSAY,
BRUNO AND PART OF THE CATCH

JIM AND LINDSAY SAWING FIREWOOD AT WABABIMIGA

LINDSAY, SENIOR, WITH A PARTICULARLY FINE MOOSE HEAD

THE VANDERBECKS' LOG HOUSE AT NAKINA

OPEN WATER! ICE THAWING IN SPRING AT THE FOOT OF SQUAW LAKE

LINDSAY PUTS HIS BACK INTO IT, POLING UP THE SQUAW

EVENING, WABABIMIGA LAKE

were accustomed to poling proved too swift. As a consequence, the early dark caught them half a dozen miles short of their intended stopping place, and they had to make camp at the head of a portage. There was a good-sized fall in the river just below them, and the roar of the water was a lullaby on which they soon drifted off to slumber.

With the first gray light of morning Jim woke to hear another sound outside, close by the wall of the tent. A loud *chump-chump*, like the gnawing of an enormous rat. He stuck his head out the tent flap and beheld some sort of black, bristling monster chewing away at the corner of the grub box.

"Hey! Get out, you!" he shouted at the top of his lungs. But the big, dark shape showed no signs of alarm. If anything, it went to work more deliberately. Heedless of the snow on his bare feet, Jim rushed forth and grabbed a heavy stick. He had lifted it high for a mortal blow when he realized that the intruder was nothing but a big porcupine. Disgusted, he lowered his weapon and caught the animal with a hearty poke amidships.

The porcupine looked around hastily, its stupid black face comic with pained surprise. Then it swung its unwieldy body and waddled off at a slow pace toward the nearest tree.

Lindsay had been watching the affair with glee. "Look out he don't spring at you," he laughed. "Bears are mighty dangerous this time o' year!"

"Oh, shut up," Jim answered sheepishly. "I knew all the time it wasn't a bear. Just wanted to keep him out o' the provisions—that was all."

He returned to the tent, rubbed his chilled toes with a blanket-cloth coat, and got into his clothes.

They pushed on up the river, stopping only a few minutes at Jim's main camp. The rim of ice along the shores had widened in the night and no words were needed to urge them on. They were racing with winter in deadly earnest.

A southwest wind was blowing when they reached Squaw Lake, and they bucked into the teeth of it, paddling hard for nearly three hours. Finally, near midafternoon, they pulled abreast of the little camp where they had left the fish and moose meat, ten days before.

To their joy the cache was safe. It required only a few minutes to stow the frozen cargo in the canoe and set off down the lake once more.

"Here," said Jim, as a big wave nearly swamped the stern of the boat, "what's the use of working, with a wind like this? Give me a hand with that tarpaulin."

They tied two corners to Lindsay's paddle and lashed it to the top of a setting pole. This they set up against the forward thwart. The wind filled their improvised sail and, with Jim steering in the stern, they went careering along at a six-mile clip.

That night they stayed at Lindsay's lower cabin, a

mile or two from the foot of the lake. Their sacks of potatoes, stored inside the camp, had not yet frozen. But if they wanted to keep them for winter they had a job to do. All evening, by the light of a candle, they peeled potatoes till their fingers were raw. In the morning, Jim got up at five to build a big fire outside. And for several hours they continued to peel and boil the tubers, till their whole supply was cooked. As soon as they came off the fire they were mashed and packed away tightly in the ten-pound tins they had brought for the purpose. Lacking a cold-proof cellar, this was the only way potatoes could be kept edible in a trapping camp.

"There, thank goodness," sighed Jim at noon, "that's over with. Now we've got just time to make Grave Lake before night."

"What!" Lindsay cried. "Do we have to start today? I'm ready for a rest."

Jim was tired too, but he shook his head. "What day is this?" he asked. "Twenty-third, isn't it? And we told Ma we'd help 'em move to Waba on the twenty-fifth. That's about the last we'll be able to use the canoes, so if you'd rather *walk* in, carrying a winter's provisions, just say the word!"

"Ouch!" said the younger boy ruefully. "No thanks. I'm ready to start as soon as you are."

Luckily the wind had gone down in the night and they encountered fairly easy paddling on the way back toward civilization. They traveled light, leaving Jim's canoe at the foot of Squaw Lake, for there were other craft stored at Nakina.

All that they carried, besides their sleeping equipment, guns and a few provisions, was Lindsay's half of the canned potatoes. These they left at his headquarters cabin on Poplar Lake next morning, and shoved on to reach town before dark.

Mrs. Vanderbeck welcomed them home with open arms, and they sat down to a supper that made their mouths water, after two weeks of woods fare. The women folk had completed their preparations for the journey to Wababimiga, and would be ready to start next day. To complete the family's good cheer, a letter had come that morning from Big Lindsay, in Toronto. It was full of his old drolleries—a letter that really sounded like himself. He was getting well so fast, he said, that they might see him packing up the track from Long Lac any day now. All he needed to build him up was a few moose steaks, and he'd sent his nurse out to get some. At any rate, the doctor said he ought to be ready to travel by the middle of November.

That night the boys carried some bags of clothing and other personal belongings down to the storehouse. They looked up the owner of the truck and engaged his services for the next morning. Finally they went to the station and collected a few packages that had come in from the mail-order house on the evening train.

As soon as breakfast was over, on the 25th, the house was closed in a bustle of departure. One of the toughest jobs was getting the dogs moved. Jim and Lindsay unchained them from the poles in front of their kennels and coaxed and hauled them out to the railroad line. Then, barking and frisking and tangling the chains, they dragged the boys pell-mell down the track. A miscellaneous pack of town dogs gathered at their approach, and Jim had to beat them off with a club to prevent a battle royal.

Fortunately the truck was waiting, with Mrs. Vanderbeck on the front seat beside the driver, and the girls sitting on the provisions, which they had loaded themselves. It was a comparatively easy matter to pile the dogs in the rear of the truck and climb up after them. Then, with a clamor that could be heard a mile, the whole menagerie set out for the lake.

They traveled in four canoes. Mrs. Vanderbeck and Mary took one, each of the boys paddled alone, and Ida, as capable a canoeman as any of them, handled a 16-footer by herself. The duffel and the dogs were distributed among the four craft and they were ready to shove off.

Fortunately it was a clear, pleasant day, with a light wind blowing from the south. They sped along down the lake, singing at the paddles. The portages took time, for it was necessary to make two or three trips over each one. However, they got to Poplar Lake in time for a late lunch and pushed on cheerfully, through the afternoon. This was a trip they always enjoyed. Ever since the children were small, they had spent their winters deep in the bush. Living was cheaper there, where game was plentiful, and the family camp was handy to the trap-lines on which so much of their livelihood depended.

The route to Wababimiga lay to the eastward, down a chain of small lakes. There was one long carry of a mile and three-quarters, and dusk was falling when Jim and Lindsay staggered over it with the last load.

"Let's go on and camp at High Hill Portage," Ida called. "We can see to paddle that far and there's no good camping ground here."

They went down an L-shaped lake in the gathering dark, and landed at the foot of a formidable looking trail that mounted straight upward 200 feet to the top of a wooded ridge. The girls pitched the two tents while the boys cut wood and built the fire, and their mother busied herself with supper getting.

It was a jolly family that sat around the blazing logs that night. Jim and Lindsay had tall tales to tell about their adventures down the Squaw, and the girls gave their own accounts of events that had taken place in Nakina.

The cold shut down in the still air, and all night long

the ice crystals were forming at the edge of the ponds. It was a desperate undertaking to pack the duffel and provisions up the frozen hill next morning. After a few futile attempts to carry the canoes, Jim decided there was enough snow to drag them up. They reached the top without mishap and were soon marching down the more gradual descent on the other side.

It was necessary to break ice to launch their flotilla in the cove at the head of Lake Wababimiga. However, the sun was bright overhead, and the steady swing of the paddles was exercise enough to keep them warm. Once out in the big lake, on the final lap of their trip, everybody's spirits rose. Ahead of them stretched mile on mile of broad water, sapphire blue and glinting in the sun. Above the white thread of snow at the shore line rose the spruces—a dark and savage host lifting feathered spears.

"There are your neighbors, Ma," called Jim, as they entered the channel between a large island and the shore. "Joe Leake's cabin—over there—see?"

He was pointing at a tiny clearing on the shore, where a wisp of smoke was rising from a ragged log hut.

"Yes," she answered. "They'll pay us a call soon enough, I expect."

It still lacked an hour of noon when they finished their eight-mile paddle and pulled in alongside the pole landing dock. Sun shone on the generous open space before the cabin and glinted from its snowy roof.

"Home again! Hurrah for old Waba!" cried Ida in sheer exuberance of spirits, and they all turned to with a will to unload the canoes.

*　　*　　*　　*

There was plenty to be done around the camp before they were settled. Jim and Lindsay chained the dogs in their winter quarters behind the cabin, then cut a few trees to add to the supply of wood. The girls rigged the stovepipe, started the fire, and brought fresh boughs for the beds. By nightfall, when the kerosene lamp was lighted, the big log room was as cozy as if it had been lived in a month.

The boys did a few final chores for their mother next morning and bade the family and each other good-by.

Lindsay was loading his canoe for the trip back to his trapping grounds on Poplar Lake. Jim filled a pack-sack, tied his bed-roll and round toed fall snowshoes on top, picked up his ax and rifle and was ready to start overland for his own territory.

The day was gray and threatening, with occasional drifting flakes of snow. Jim hiked along steadily through the bush, following a line of old blazes he had made two years before. Five or six miles due north from Wababimiga he came out on the shore of a smaller body of water. It was Porcupine Lake, where he planned to set a trap-line. Making a circuit of the shore, he patched up some of last year's cubbies as he went. And before night he reached a little, rough pole camp with a bough roof, which would serve him as a shelter if it began snowing in earnest.

He looked out across the chill, gray lake before he built his supper fire. There was no charm in that landscape. No grandeur of hills. No peaceful beauty of fields. Only the dark, savage woods and the water, and the relentless winter sky. He was the only human thing in that immensity of wilderness. Lonesome? A little. But not afraid. As he stretched his arms and shoulders he felt a tingling sense of well-being. He was ready to pit his youth and strength and woodsman's skill against the challenge of the North.

The little lean-to had an open front, facing toward the embers of the fire. Lying there in his sleeping-bag he could hear all the noises of the night. The scurry of chipmunks—the thudding hop of a snowshoe rabbit— then, far away, the hoot of a hunting owl. Somewhere on the other side of the lake a fox yelped sharply. The silence seemed to thicken after that, and just before he fell asleep he caught the faint rustle and hiss of snow falling softly on the evergreen roof.

Several inches had been added to the white blanket when he rose, at daylight. It would be a clear day, but bad traveling. He got breakfast, finished his work along the trap-line, and set out westward for Squaw Lake.

It was a good six miles straight through the bush, with soft muskeg and a series of sharp, rocky ridges to vary the monotony. There were no blaze marks to follow but Jim had been through the country before and was able to keep his bearings by the sun. The snow, not yet deep enough for snowshoeing, made the going heavy. It was late in the afternoon when he came to the lake shore, and darkening fast when he reached his canoe. After two days afoot, the easy motion of paddling was a relief.

He crossed to Lindsay's lower camp, spent the night there, and in the morning set out down Squaw River. The water had gone down a little and he shot the rapids safely. So, at noon on the 29th of October, he returned to his own main camp, ready for the real business of the winter. In three days the trapping season would begin.

Ermine

VI

THE trap-line Jim had laid out for himself was close to seventy-five miles in extent. Over this broad stretch of woods and water he would have absolute domain for the next seven months.

The line ran from his home camp thirty miles or more down the Squaw to the lower camp he had visited with Lindsay. Thence it doubled back up the river as far as Beaver Lake portage. From Beaver Lake there was a trail south to Porcupine River, and he planned to have traps all the way up this stream to Porcupine Lake. From there the trail led northward to Whitefish

Lake and so back to his home cabin.

Lindsay's line was shorter but still a big territory for a sixteen-year-old to cover. Its route was down Poplar Lake, through Grave Lake and upper Squaw Lake, then across to Sucker Lake and back into the lower end of Squaw Lake. The round trip would take in about forty miles.

Jim rose very early, the morning of the 30th, and set out before daybreak for Whitefish Lake. From its northern end he cut through the bush on foot, and followed the bank of Porcupine River for several hours. A little after noon he found what he was looking for—a camping site close to the stream.

The boy built a small fire and ate a few mouthfuls of cold lunch, washing them down with a cup of tea. Then he spit on his hands and picked up the ax. In the next hour he felled and trimmed half a dozen straight spruce poles, cut them into even lengths and began notching the ends for a log house. The cabin he built was extremely simple. It had no windows, and one whole side was open. The roof was made of small poles, notched and held in place with nails he had brought in his pack-sack. When a thick layer of boughs had been laid over them in the form of thatch, and the crevices had been chinked with moss, he had a stout and fairly weather-tight shelter.

The cabin was not finished till well into the morning of the next day, and he had to push along steadily

to cover the fifteen miles back to his home camp by
nightfall. The weather had been milder the last two
days. A red-streaked sunset promised another fair day
on the morrow, and he looked forward eagerly to setting his traps. If no more ice formed he would be able
to use the canoe.

Jim got up long before dawn. By the time the first
gray lightened the east he had dressed, built his fire
and eaten a hasty breakfast. Then, stowing his rifle, ax,
showshoes, bed-roll, a few supplies and a bag of frozen
fish in the canoe, he pushed off down the river. By now
he had an accurate plan of the whole trap-line in his
mind, and he needed to waste no time in hunting for
the cubbies. Pulling in to shore at the first one, he tied
a piece of fish five or six inches above the end of the
slanting approach log, then pushed down the spring
of the trap and set the trigger. When the open trap
was laid in a notch at the top of the log he sprinkled
the pan with a dusting of light snow. His hands, in
skin mittens rubbed with oil from rat musks, left no
human scent.

Working as fast as possible, he moved on from one
cubby to the next, along both banks of the river. Sometimes the traps were only a little distance apart. Again,
he might cover a mile or more without coming to a
trap-house. At noon he cast a hurried glance aloft and
saw a leaden, cold sky all the way to the horizon. No
time to eat lunch. He went on setting traps till the first

flakes of the storm whirled by on a sudden gust of wind. About three in the afternoon it started to snow in earnest. The sky, the hurrying river and the bush, all were blotted out in a swirling veil of white.

Jim was nearing the head of the Long Portage. He made one or two more sets, hampered by the blinding snow, and steered his canoe across the current, paddling more by instinct than by sight. A short distance from the end of the carry there was a little camp—a pole and bark lean-to that would give him some sort of shelter from the storm. He hauled the canoe out and over- turned it, carrying his duffel up the bank. To his joy there was a good-sized pile of firewood in the lee of the hut.

The lean-to had one open side that faced south, out of the wind. A few yards away there was a huge butt log, half burned through. Jim shaved a dry stick of pine with his knife, laid a heap of split kindling beside it, and sheltered the flame of a match under his macki- naw. The tiny blaze struggled with the snow and wind, sank almost to nothing, then flared again and caught in the shavings. He fed the fire, stick by stick, till it was strong enough to hold its own. When it was roar- ing hungrily, he went back into the woods and cut another dead tree. Plenty of fuel was a first essential in an open camp. He would have to keep the fire up all night.

Fresh boughs for the bed came next, and then sup-

per. He toasted some bread, made a kettle of cocoa
and opened a can of corned beef hash for the occasion.
After he had eaten he sat for a while in the door of his
shelter and watched the hissing flames. He was warm
and out of the wind. The red glow of the fire lighted
a narrow circle walled by steadily falling snow. It was
like a cozy room, completely shut off from the night
and the storm.

When he grew sleepy, Jim piled logs on the blaze and
crawled into his eiderdown. He woke twice in the
night to look at the fire and put on more wood. A sort
of woodsman's sixth sense roused him when this was
necessary.

There was no real dawn next morning—simply a
graying of the night to show dim outlines of trees
through the snow-filled air.

Jim whistled to keep up his spirits as he rebuilt the
fire. It was too bad—this storm at the very beginning
of the season, when every day counted. Still, you had
to learn patience if you were a trapper. Weather was
something that couldn't be hurried.

He spent the day as best he could, mending a break
in one of his snowshoes, cutting more wood, cooking
himself sparing meals. His provisions were beginning
to run low.

That night, just before he drowsed off to sleep, there
came a change. The wind eddied lightly across the door
of the hut and he saw a star twinkling through the

trees. The storm was over.

Jim rose early, eager to be off. When he pushed his ax handle into the dry snow, it sank down to within a few inches of the head. Two feet deep. He went to the river for a kettle of water and saw slush blocking the current. That was bad. He knew the canoe would hardly move in that sluggish mass. Nevertheless, when he had eaten he launched the craft and made a try at it.

No use. The bow crept forward a few yards, driven by powerful strokes of the paddle, then came to a standstill. The narrow lane of water behind him closed up again, and he had to labor for five minutes to regain the bank. There was nothing for it but to haul out the canoe and put on his snowshoes.

Jim had used almost the last of his food for breakfast. He would have to get back to his home camp and leave the lower end of the line unset. As the sun rose it grew warmer and the snow was soft and sticky. The boy plodded up along the shore, zigzagging to avoid thickets and making his own trail as he went. Such traps as he passed were still undisturbed. Once or twice he found the bait stolen—probably by those perennial thieves, the gorbies. But no fur-bearers had ventured out during the storm.

Leg-weary and wet with perspiration, Jim hauled in at his main camp just before sunset. The first thing he did was to heat a kettle of water and give himself a sketchy bath. A change of underwear felt good, and a supper of fried moose meat and potatoes made his physical comfort complete.

In the night he woke to hear heavy drops drumming on the roof. A steady, warm rain fell on the camp all the next day, melting the snow and raising the level of the water. When Jim rose on the morning of the fifth, he found the air clear and sharp, and the river no longer clogged with slush. It was a day for action. He packed his knap-sack with provisions and set out down the shore once more.

This time the going was better. The snow, packed down by the rain and thinly crusted over, gave firmer footing. He looked at the traps again as he went. In the first five or six there was no sign of fur. Then he saw a narrow track, frozen in the crust, leading toward one of his cubbies. Too small for a mink, but he followed eagerly. When the snow covered trap-house came in sight, he thought at first there was nothing in it. Then, against the blanket of white he saw two tiny black specks. An ermine, caught by both forelegs, was glaring at him with steady hate in its shoe-button eyes. The slim white body, blending perfectly with the snow, had been invisible at five paces. He killed it with a quick, merciful blow on the skull, put the limp body in his pack-sack, and reset the trap.

Before he reached the lean-to at the head of the portage he was rewarded by two more of the little white weasels. Not a big day's catch, but at least a start. There was enough daylight left to carry the canoe over the two-mile trail and return to the shelter to sleep.

It grew steadily colder in the night. Jim found the water in his teakettle frozen to a solid block of ice when he started to get breakfast. The temperature must be down to zero or below. He packed the rest of his duffel on his back and hurried across the portage.

The current was running fast below the rapids, and there was still open water three or four feet from the bank. Jim got the canoe in and started down. He set the first half dozen traps without much difficulty, but two miles below he came to a pool where the river was frozen from shore to shore. He succeeded in breaking a path through the thin ice and hauled out in the snow. A half mile hike along the bank showed him that it was useless to go further in the canoe. The big freeze had come at last. He would be lucky to get his craft back to the portage. Hurrying on, afoot, he set traps as far as he dared, along the north side of the river. The cubbies on the other shore would have to go untended for a while.

It was late when Jim paddled the last few strokes that sent the bow up on the ice at the foot of the long carry. He lifted the canoe to his shoulders and hastened along the rapidly darkening trail. Tired, hungry and cold, he slid and stumbled on the icy footing. That two miles had never seemed so long. When he thought he had made half the carry he set down his load for a minute's rest.

A windless night, still and sharp. Across the southwest sky there was still a dull glow of red, and against it the spruce branches hung in inky black silhouette. Miles away through the silent bush, he heard a coyote howl. A shiver shook him.

"Huh!" he grunted, disgusted with himself. "Might think I was a greenhorn—gettin' the shakes when a little brush-wolf hollers!"

He swung the canoe up again and plodded on. When he reached the cabin the stars were out.

*   *   *   *

More and more of the river was frozen over, as Jim hiked westward next morning. At one place he was able to cross over on the new ice, so clear and black that he could see the boulders in the stream bed beneath him. In this way he looked at his traps along the south bank on his route to the main camp. Two ermine were added to the three already in his pack, and in the last trap he visited he found the frozen body of a mink. This was a real catch—a big fellow in prime fur.

Jim felt its deep, silky softness and figured he could get twelve or thirteen dollars for that pelt.

As he neared his home camp he was watching the

river for another stretch of solid ice. He still had to get back to the north side. Up ahead he saw a place where the stream seemed to be frozen across, but to reach it he had to circle off to the left around a dense spruce thicket that lined the bank. It was just as he came in sight of the river again that he saw something moving among the trees on the far shore. The boy stood still as a statue, all his senses alert. A couple of hundred yards upstream a big grayish-brown shape drifted out of the shadow of the woods. It walked out on the frozen river, lifting splay hoofs daintily. Huge antlers thrust upward and backward from its head, and its nose was raised to test the wind.

Jim had seen caribou before, but never as close as this one. An old bull, he judged, from the strong neck and the sweep of gray-white mane. He held his breath as two more caribou followed their leader onto the ice. They were smaller and lighter in build, with a narrower spread of antlers—a pair of cows. The cow caribou, he remembered, was different from all other members of the deer family. She grew horns after the first year and never shed them.

The boy did not stir till all three had made their way across the frozen surface. Caribou were protected game, but he couldn't help casting a regretful look after them. The big bull had offered a tempting mark for a rifle.

[66]

Continuing up the shore, he came to the place where their tracks led off to the south. Well, his question about where to cross had been answered. He was soon on the north bank and headed for home.

Fisher

VII

THE sun was still above the trees when Jim reached his cabin. He would have time to skin his fur before dark.

The weasels were comparatively easy. A dozen tiny stretchers, made the year before, stood in a corner of the camp. They were narrow, pointed slats, tapering out to an inch or more in width at the base. When he had whetted the blade of his big jackknife, he slit the first ermine around the hind legs and worked the hide off over the head. The skin, inside out, was then pulled over a pair of stretchers, and a wedge was driven in between them to spread the pelt tight. This ended the job, since ermine skins are sold with the fur inside.

There was more science to dressing the mink. The actual removal of the skin was done in much the same way but, once on the long stretchers, the pelt was tacked down and placed on a rack outside to freeze. Jim left it there half an hour or more, while he brought in firewood and started supper. When the hide was stiffly frozen, he brought it in, took a dull case knife and scraped it clean of fat. High above the stove there was a row of poles for drying clothes. On this, Jim laid the mink hide and left it to dry for several hours. Just before bedtime he got it down and turned the pelt with the fur side out, again tacking down the legs and tail. The mink skin would stay on the stretcher two or three more days, till the nose grew hard. This was the accepted sign that the fur was cured.

According to Jim's reckoning the next morning was the eighth of November. A full week had passed and less than half his traps were set. However the weather remained clear and cold, and he meant to make the most of it.

Filling his pack with rations for several days, he made a bundle of fish for bait, took his bed-roll, ax and rifle, and crossed the river on the ice. In a few moments he had picked up the blazes on the trail to Whitefish Lake.

It was a sparkling, bright day when the sun came up. Well below freezing, but not too cold to work along the trail in comfort. As he came to each cubby, Jim set his trap methodically and pushed on without wasting time. Four or five whisky-jacks followed in his wake, attracted by the fish. Their constant scolding kept him company for several miles, until he turned and caught one of the birds trying to steal the bait out of a trap-house. With a growl of righteous wrath, Jim brought up his rifle and blew the marauder into eternity. After that they left him in peace for a while.

As he crossed the portage from Whitefish to Porcupine Lake he saw the snow dotted everywhere with the tracks of snowshoe rabbits. It looked like a good rabbit year, and that meant a good season for fisher and fox. It was, he remembered, four winters since the last plague. Every seventh year the rabbits multiplied to such numbers that a disease spread among them and killed them by the thousand. Then all game became scarce. Most of the fur-bearers were too wise to touch a sick rabbit, and so, in the plague years, they either starved or migrated out of the country.

Twice the trail was crossed by the clean, dainty prints of foxes, and half a mile farther on Jim came to a fisher track. He took special pains with the traps along that part of the line, setting the bait high and making sure that the clogs were heavy enough to hold a large animal.

He made no stop for lunch but plodded steadily along the shore of Porcupine Lake. The whole surface of the pond was a solid sheet of four-inch ice, and he crossed at the eastern end without difficulty. From there he worked on down the outlet stream, reaching the new Porcupine River camp just as dusk was falling.

It was the coldest night so far that winter. Even with a roaring fire reflecting its heat into the lean-to, and the thick, soft folds of the eiderdown wrapping his body, Jim had trouble keeping warm.

He was up before dawn and ready for the trail. All day he set traps down the Porcupine and got back to the lean-to only at supper-time. To vary the monotony of his diet he had shot a couple of rabbits, and with their meager flesh he prepared a rather flat tasting stew that night. He ate it more from a sense of duty than from appetite.

"Needs an onion," he remarked to himself. "Don't know how foxes and such get to like rabbit without onions."

Being alone in the woods for weeks on end was no new experience for Jim. It was one of the hardships of winter trapping that one simply had to get used to. He missed Lindsay and their good-natured brotherly arguments. When he was busy, the solitude wasn't so bad, but at night, between supper and bed, he had to invent ways of occupying himself. Sometimes he whistled or hummed the tunes of old plantation songs. Stephen Foster's melodies are as much loved in Canada as in the South, and Jim's favorites were "Swanee

888

River," "Darling Nellie Gray," and "Old Black Joe."

More satisfying still was the fun of reciting poetry. During his brief sessions at the little school in Nakina, Jim had gotten hold of a collection of Robert W. Service's poems. There was a rugged, masculine ring to the lines that stirred the boy's imagination. He liked their rough Northern background and the adventurous stories they told. Most of them he had learned by heart. Striding along the trail or sitting by his campfire, he could reel off whole pages of "The Shooting of Dan McGrew" and other frontier sagas with hardly a pause for breath.

Tonight, after he had stirred up the fire against the cold and thrown on a couple of big logs, he squatted in the entrance of the lean-to and declaimed "Men of the High North" to the mounting flames.

"Can you remember your huskies all going,
    Barking with joy and their brushes in air;
You in your parka, glad-eyed and glowing,
    Monarch, your subjects the wolf and the bear?

"Monarch, your kingdom unravisht and gleaming;
    Mountains your throne, and a river your car;
Crash of a bull moose to rouse you from dreaming;
    Forest your couch, and your candle a star—"

The words died in his throat. Somewhere off to the right he had heard a sudden sharp crackle of brush.

For long seconds he crouched there listening. Then, so close it made him shiver, came the quavering howl of a hunting wolf. It was repeated, a moment later from farther away, and then two voices together took up the cry. There was a panting eagerness in those howls. The wolves were moving fast, and they must have been on a hot trail or they would never have passed so near his camp.

Jim snatched up his rifle and ran to the river bank. There were stars overhead, but no moon. The ice stretched dim and ghostly to right and left. He turned west, in the direction from which he had heard the sounds, and went swiftly along in the shadow of the woods. After a minute or two he came to a bend in the shore line, beyond which he remembered the stream widened to a small pond. For the next few steps his view of the river ahead was cut off by a clump of spruces, but even before he had passed them he knew the end of the hunt was near. A new noise had reached him through the trees—a snarling, breathless noise of struggle.

He gripped the rifle tighter and ran forward, till the ice-covered pool spread out before him. In the middle of this open space, not thirty yards away, he saw a huddled dark mass around which gray shadows circled and feinted. Three caribou stood at bay, their rumps close together, their lowered antlers forming a loose, shifting ring of defense. Just out of reach the wolves galloped and whirled, trying desperately to breach that wall of tossing horns. As the boy watched, two of the gray killers made a snarling rush at one of the smaller caribou, and a third, waiting his opening, leaped in to take the harassed deer on the flank. While the attacker was still in mid-spring he was caught by a lightninglike swing of the big bull's antlers and tossed a dozen feet.

Jim had already leveled the Winchester. When the wolf landed on the ice, half stunned, he took a quick sight and pulled the trigger. At the crack of the report, four huge gray shapes raced for the bush. The fifth lay in a still, sprawled heap where the bullet had stopped him.

As the boy moved out toward the middle of the pond, the caribou bull lifted his muzzle into the wind and gave a long, whistling snort. Then he shouldered his cows toward the far bank and trotted off behind them in triumph.

Jim circled the gray body cautiously. When he was certain the beast was dead he took hold of one of the hind legs and dragged it behind him to camp. The light of the fire showed him a good-sized timber wolf, full furred but gaunt with hunger. The blunt, clublike points of the caribou's horns had done no damage to the hide, but the rifle bullet had broken the animal's neck and nearly taken the head off.

Late as it was, Jim slung the wolf on a pole and

skinned him. He was well satisfied with his night's work. The pelt would be worth something in addition to the $25 bounty. And in the thrill of the fight he had just witnessed, his sympathies had been all with the caribou. They seemed like old friends, for he had no doubt it was the same herd he had seen crossing the Squaw, two days before.

*   *   *   *

The bitter cold had abated somewhat by the next morning, but it was still clear, and the light wind promised continued fair weather. Jim made good time on the trail to Porcupine Lake and back to his home camp. There was no fur in his traps, though one of them held a snowshoe rabbit, and the gorbies had filched the bait from a couple of others. Since his fish were exhausted, he cut up the rabbit and rebaited the traps with meat.

It was only a little past noon when Jim reached his cabin. There were many chores to be done around the place, and he set to work at once. First a roaring fire had to be built in the stove. He had a craving for fresh bread and, while the cylindrical oven, built into the stovepipe, was heating up, he mixed a batch of dough.

Next he set a big pan of snow on the fire and laid out his clothes to be washed. The laundry work and a bit of mending took the rest of the afternoon. The delicious odor of baking bread filled the cabin and sent the jays outside into a frenzy of jealous scolding. When

[75]

the first loaf came out of the oven, Jim cut himself a generous slice and stood in the door, laughing at his ruffled neighbors while he ate it.

That night he straightened up the camp and replenished his pack-sack. He and Lindsay had agreed to meet in two weeks, when they parted at Wababimiga. Tomorrow would be the fourteenth day, and Jim meant to get an early start up river.

Only about eight miles lay between his cabin and Lindsay's lower camp, but he found several of the faster flowing stretches of the river were still unfrozen, and it was necessary to make detours along the shore. Just before noon he came out on the ice at the foot of Squaw Lake, and headed for his brother's shack. There was no smoke coming from the stovepipe, and he heard no answer to his hail. Opening the door, he looked inside. The fire was out and Lindsay's gun and snowshoes were gone.

Jim picked up what looked like the freshest trail among the maze of tracks in front of the camp. It led off westward, up the lake.

Mile by mile, as he swung along, Jim watched the shore for a glimpse of a moving figure. He knew Lindsay might be working anywhere on the trap-line. But it wasn't till late afternoon, when he had covered ten more miles and was nearing the head of the lake, that he saw a dark speck ahead on the ice. He flung up his arm and the other figure waved in answer. As they shortened the distance between them, he could see Lindsay's sturdy shoulders hunched under his pack, and what looked like a stuffed black stocking draped around his ears.

"Hi, kid!" he shouted. "What's that hanging round your neck?"

Lindsay only grinned and plodded nearer. When he was a few strides away he reached up a free hand and pulled a big, dark, furry animal off the top of the pack.

"Sa-a-ay!" cried Jim. "A fisher! Boy, are you lucky!"

Lindsay was beaming. "Just got him an hour ago," he said. "Up in that cubby at the head of Clam River. I had a No. 4 set there and a rabbit for bait. He was in clear up to the shoulder."

A fisher is the trapper's prize catch. It is a slim, long-bodied animal, with a head somewhat like a cat's, and a sleek tail, tapering to a point. Unlike the mink, it is a land animal, living on rabbits and other small game. Its habits are like those of its cousin, the marten, though it is larger and finer furred. In color it may run all the way from brown or dark gray to jet-black.

Jim ruffled the silky brown fur admiringly. "Too bad he's not a couple o' shades darker," he remarked. "Be worth a lot o' money if he was a black one."

"Say—I'm not kickin'!" Lindsay answered stoutly. "How many fisher have *you* got, Big Shot?"

Jim laughed, "All right, I'm just jealous, I reckon,"

he admitted. "Tell me—how's everything? Where were you in all that snow?"

"Right there in my lower camp. I was coming down from Sucker Lake when it started. I s'pose you were off down river somewhere."

"Yeah—in that lean-to at the long carry," Jim answered. "Listen—we don't want to hike all the way back. Let's sleep up here at the little camp tonight. I've got enough grub."

They turned toward the sunset and soon reached the half wall and tent they had put up while they were netting fish. It was dry and clean inside, and when they threw back the front flap and built a good fire before the opening, it didn't take long to make the place comfortable.

"All right," said Jim, when the firewood and fresh bedding had been brought. "I'll get the supper. You start in right at the beginning and tell me everything that's happened."

Lindsay's two weeks had been fairly uneventful. He had all his traps set, and his catch of fur was running about the same as Jim's. Half a dozen ermine, a pine marten, and the fisher which he was skinning while he talked. He had seen nobody, though he had come across the track of a sled on Poplar Lake the day before.

"Four dogs, looked like, and all about the same size. Not a very heavy man. I figured it was Emile Coté," he said.

"I guess likely," Jim nodded. "He told me he'd be going to town for the mail about now. Wonder if he had a letter from Dad. Well, I'll soon know. In a couple of days I've got to head for Waba and get me a dog team."

VIII

THE two boys put in the following day going up to Poplar Lake, loading up with provisions from the supply left at Lindsay's home camp, and walking back to the foot of Squaw Lake. Jim spent the night there in his brother's shack and then hit the trail for his own camp on Squaw River. His shoulders were sore from the heavy packing. With the dogs he could load a sled and make better time on the trails. For that reason he decided to let the lower trap-line go until after he had made a trip to Wababimiga.

He set out the morning of the 14th, traveling light. There were six inches or so of new snow, fallen in the night, and already the white surface was written over with the signatures of a score of different animals and birds. The morning was fair, the air cold but dry and bracing. He swung along like a young bull moose, glad to be alive.

Half way up Porcupine Lake he had a feeling of being followed. When he glanced back he saw three timber wolves trotting along his track, a hundred yards in the rear. They stopped the instant he turned and stood there watching him with inscrutable yellow eyes.

"Gosh," he muttered to himself, "what a sap I was not to bring the rifle. I could drill that front one just as easy—"

He had left the .32 at home in its deerskin case, thinking he could travel faster if he didn't have to carry it. And here was forty dollars' worth of pelt and bounty begging to be taken! He wondered if the wolves realized that he had no gun. They sure were bold about it, trailing him that way! Slowly he raised his ax, aiming the handle as he would a rifle barrel, but there was no scurrying to cover among the wolves. The only movement he could see was the slow waving of the leader's brush.

"Can't fool you, can I?" Jim grinned, and plodded ahead up the lake. He didn't bother to look back for another half mile. When he did the gray trackers had disappeared.

Jim rarely bothered with a noonday meal unless he happened to be in camp. He had eaten a good breakfast that morning, and now he pushed ahead through the brief northern daylight without a pause. On the shore of the little pond to the south of Porcupine he came on a roughly fashioned trap-house. At first glance he thought it might have been built by his sisters, for the place was only five or six miles from their cabin on Wababimiga. There was a red fox dead in the trap. Jim went closer, and was on the point of taking the animal out, when he noticed the bait. It was moose meat. And the trap itself was an old-fashioned double-spring affair, unlike any of the Vanderbecks' equipment. He remembered then—that Hudson Bay Indian, Joe Leake. The Cree must be trapping this ground.

A tremendous barking heralded Jim's approach to the home cabin. The dogs had seen him coming across the cove through the naked hardwoods of the clearing. Then he caught sight of Ida waving to him from the doorway and quickened his pace to a trot.

It was good to strip off his mackinaw and heavy sweater and bask in the warmth of the homelike room. Good, too, to hear the women folks' chatter and sit down to a heaping plate of his mother's cooking.

Yes, they told him, there had been a letter from Toronto, brought through by Emile. Big Lindsay would be coming home soon—in a week perhaps—and had arranged with a man in Nakina to carry him to Waba with a fast team of dogs.

After supper Jim brought in enough wood to last them a day or two, and then settled himself to read a magazine, reveling in the luxury of the kerosene lamp.

His mother and the girls were sewing and mending around the table.

Hardly had they made themselves comfortable when their peace was shattered by a furious turmoil rising from the dog huts.

"Must be an animal back there," said Jim, getting up. "That, or someone coming."

At that moment there was a rustle of snowshoes outside and a knock on the door. "Come in," called Mrs. Vanderbeck. As the latch lifted and the heavy door creaked open, Jim saw a small, squat Indian in a greasy canvas coat, a shapeless black felt hat pulled down on his ears.

His beady little dark eyes shifted from the women to Jim, and his feet hesitated for a bare fraction of a second, though his seamed face did not change expression.

"Come in, Joe Leake, and shut the door," Mrs. Vanderbeck repeated curtly. But with a man in the house, the Indian seemed to feel it improper to return her greeting. He nodded his head solemnly to Jim, then turned and spoke a gruff word in Cree to something behind him. A little Indian boy of nine or ten darted across the threshold like a scared rabbit, and Joe Leake closed the door.

Jim indicated the end of the puncheon bench. "Sit down," he said. "You got a pipe? Here—smoke."

He brought a can of his father's Navy Cut from the

shelf, and watched the man fill a dirty old briar pipe, taken from his pocket. Refusing the match Jim offered, the Indian leaned down to the wood-box for a splinter of pine and lit it through an opening in the stove. He drew four or five slow puffs, savoring the aroma of the good tobacco. Then, ceremoniously, he offered the pipe to Jim.

The boy suppressed a shudder and took the blackened thing in steady fingers. He managed a couple of gentle pulls as a matter of etiquette, and handed it back. Now the conversation could proceed.

"Boy," said Joe, after a moment of polite silence, "him sick."

Jim looked at the ragged urchin in some alarm, but there were no red spots or other signals of contagion on his grimy copper skin.

"What's the matter with him?" he asked.

The Cree's words of explanation were few, but he made himself entirely plain. Mrs. Vanderbeck's motherly interest was aroused. "Hm," she murmured, rising from her chair, "a good dose o' castor oil is what he needs."

While she was getting the bottle and an old pewter spoon, Joe Leake explained the failure of his own favorite tribal remedy.

"Me peelum bark jack-pine," he said, "Boy lickum. Too cold. No sap. No good."

"Here, youngster," said Mrs. Vanderbeck kindly.

"Take a spoonful o' this."

The Indian growled something in Cree and pushed the boy forward. Jim watched him with amusement as the spoon neared his open mouth. His black eyes shone with something between fear and excitement. He was having an adventure. The viscous stuff was in his mouth now. He looked surprised but gulped it down manfully and made no outcries or faces.

"There," beamed Jim's mother. "I think he'll be all right now."

Joe Leake seemed pleased. He jerked a finger at the bottle.

"Me gettum big medicine at store," he said. "What name callum?"

Jim got a scrap of paper and fished the stub of a pencil out of his pocket. "Here," he laughed. "I'll write it for you. You just ask the man at the store in Nakina for a bottle of that." And he laid the pencil on the bench, handing the prescription to the Indian.

Joe Leake folded it with some care and deposited it in his shirt pocket. Only then did his face crack into a smile, and he nodded his thanks to Mrs. Vanderbeck. Seizing the youngster by the wrist he was about to depart when Jim stopped him.

"Is that your trap-line up there on the small lake?" he asked, pointing northward.

The Cree gave a grunt of assent.

"I came by there today," Jim said. "There's a fox

[85]

in your trap."

"Me go gettum tomorrow," the Indian replied briefly, and walked out with his son in dignified silence.

Jim went back to his magazine with a grin. "Didn't act very grateful about it, did he?" he remarked.

"Don't you worry," said his mother. "They don't make a show, but they're grateful enough. Poor things! Eight of 'em in that awful shack! And nothing much to live on but moose meat. No wonder they get off their feed."

"Have you been up to see the place?" Jim asked in some surprise.

"Sure. The woman paid us a call a few days after we got here, so we returned it. Never saw such a dirty hole in all my days. But there—the poor soul hasn't anything to do with. Besides, she comes from way up beyond Fort Churchill, somewhere. She's not used to civilized ways."

"An Eskimo woman," Ida put in. "I think she's better looking than any squaw I've ever seen. She's tall and straight—not fat, like I thought Eskimos were. And she's got queer eyes, sort of slanting. Emile says the track Indians are afraid of her. They think she's a witch."

"You ought to see their girl," Mary said, biting off a piece of thread. "The skinniest, forlornest little thing. They make her work all the time, scraping moose hides. How many is it Joe's killed already, this fall, Ma—

[86]

twelve or thirteen? They only bring a dollar apiece, and that poor kid has to spend days on every one, scraping away with an old shin bone to get off the hair."

"Gosh!" Jim frowned. "Killing moose at that rate is pretty bad. They let Indians have a moose a month, but a dozen of 'em in five weeks—boy, that's wicked! I'd complain about it to the game warden, only I know he doesn't like to meddle into Indian affairs. These treaty Indians are just like children. They've always killed any animal they wanted for food, and I guess that's fair enough. But the government ought to tell 'em where to stop, when it comes to slaughtering moose this way."

His mother patted his shoulder. "You quit worrying about it, son," she said. "Dear knows there's plenty of moose in this country, and I reckon one Indian won't exterminate 'em. We'll see what Dad wants to do about it when he gets here. Now it's bedtime. We've wasted enough kerosene tonight, if you remember what a job it is to pack it in here."

"All right," Jim yawned. "Just give me a couple of minutes to write up my diary." He got the little black book out of his possible-sack and reached in his pocket for the pencil stub.

"Now where the dickens did that go?" he inquired, mystified. "Oh, I remember. I left it on the bench here." But a search of the floor failed to reveal it. There were uneven cracks between the puncheons, and Jim

[87]

finally decided the pencil had slipped through one of them. He got another out of the cupboard and jotted down the events of the day in his diary. Then his mother pulled the cloth curtain that partitioned off the girls' sleeping quarters, and they all went to bed.

Jim had set the alarm clock for six. It was pitch dark, of course, when the bell woke him, but he could see the stars shining clear above the lake. He built up the fire while his mother was dressing, then put on his outdoor clothes and went to the shed behind the cabin. From the racks overhead he selected a light seven-foot toboggan. Several sets of dog harness hung on pegs, freshly oiled and supple. He took down the shortest of them—a two-dog hitch—and went over each strap and buckle, to make sure of its strength.

The collars were steel frames padded with leather. They looked exactly like miniature horse collars, except that they were rounder, to fit a dog's neck. They even had tiny steel hames at the top, where they buckled together. From a ring in either side of the collar, a trace strap led back toward the sled. The second harness in the tandem was fastened to the traces by short straps, so that the lead dog would never be pulling directly on the collar of the one behind him. And the tugs were held up by saddle straps running across each dog's back, behind the shoulders.

As soon as breakfast was eaten, Jim went up to the kennels.

The whole pack greeted him with eager whinings, and he stopped to pat each dog in turn. When he came to Pat and Bruno, he unfastened their chains from the run-poles and brought them back to the cabin.

Bruno, the big German shepherd dog, had been Jim's leader for two years. He was quick, tireless and intelligent—an ideal animal to head a team. Pat, heavier and thicker furred, was part collie and part Airedale, with a trace of St. Bernard to give him size. He lacked Bruno's nervous eagerness, but made up for it in grit and sturdy power.

The girls had loaded the sled with Jim's winter clothing, his pack-sack, ax and long winter snowshoes. A carefully wrapped bundle of his mother's biscuits and a dried-apple pie completed the cargo, and a tarpaulin was laced over the top.

Jim led Bruno to the harness and slipped the collar around his neck. At the familiar feel of it, the big dog shivered a little, looked up at his master, and wagged his tail. He knew he was going back to work. Next Pat was harnessed. He growled once and snapped at the trace strap, then stolidly submitted to fate. The young trapper settled his snowshoes, waved a good-by to the family, and stepped to the front of the team. "Hup, Bruno!" he called, and they were off.

Until they reached the single track northward from Wababimiga, Jim led the way. Then he dropped back to let Bruno follow the broken trail. The light toboggan ran smoothly and it was easier walking in its wake.

They had been moving less than an hour and had covered perhaps three miles, when Bruno halted suddenly, growling deep in his throat. Jim yelled at him to go on but the dog stayed where he was, his nose sniffing at the trail and a sharp ridge of fur rising along his back. The boy ran forward around the sled and reached the leader's side. A single glance showed him what had stopped the dog. There in the snow was a great, deep footprint, clear to the very points of the toenails. The Big Wolf had passed that way in the night.

Jim knelt and laid his open hand in the track. It was the same gigantic paw mark that he and Lindsay had seen, up on the Squaw. As he rose, the old lead dog jerked his grizzled head back and gave vent to a weird, mournful howl.

"Shut up, you fool!" Jim ordered angrily. "Might think you'd never smelled a wolf track before. Come on, now—get moving, the pair of you!"

He strode ahead and the dogs obediently came after him. It was only when they passed the frozen body of the fox in the trap a few miles farther on, that Jim thought of Joe Leake and his Eskimo witch-wife. The trail of the monster wolf had been heading straight across country toward the Indian's cabin. In spite of himself, the boy had a queer feeling.

*   *   *   *

An hour before sunset that night, they reached Jim's home camp. He had cut the logs for dog kennels before he left, and now he quickly threw up the walls, nailed the pole roofs in place and piled snow on top. By dusk the two huts were finished. He tossed a heap of spruce tips in the bottom of each and hooked the dog chains to the staples. Pat and Bruno sniffed all around their new quarters, then went inside and lay down.

Jim soon had a good fire going in the cabin stove. He put on a couple of pails of snow to melt, and cooked up a mash of corn meal and fish for the dogs while his own supper was in progress. An hour later he turned in. Tired as he was, his sleep that night was disturbed by uneasy dreams of a yellow, slant-eyed squaw who took on the shape of an enormous wolf.

The morning of the 16th dawned clear, and Jim was up betimes. The dogs needed rest after their first day's hauling, so he left them at home and spent the day cruising up a nearby brook in search of mink sign. There were few tracks but it looked like good country and he set two traps before returning to camp. He planned to start next day on the long circuit down the Squaw and up the Porcupine. With good luck he would be back inside of five days.

Mink

IX

THE trail down river was still unbroken, but six inches of light, dry snow didn't make bad going. Jim led the way, plowing a path with his snowshoes. The first few traps had nothing in them. Then he came to one that was sprung and discovered the toes of a fisher gnawed off at the jaws. Rotten luck! He reset the trap gloomily and hiked on. In the very next cubby better fortune awaited him, for he found a fine, dark mink lying frozen in the snow. It had dragged the clog a dozen yards before it caught between two tree trunks. There were two weasels in the traps below.

While Jim was visiting a cubby a few yards off the trail he heard the dogs break into sudden barking behind him. Turning, he was just in time to see a cow moose and a half-grown calf go crashing through a thicket. Pat was crazy to follow them, and an upset sled might have resulted if Jim had not yelled loudly at the team. At his voice, Bruno whirled and growled a warning that quieted the second dog.

They got to the lean-to at Long Portage well before dark. As soon as Jim had skinned his fur and cleaned up after supper, he went to bed. He meant to make a long day of it tomorrow and they would be starting hours before daylight.

The alarm clock that most good woodsmen carry in their brains roused him in the dark. He looked out at the stars and knew it must be nearly five o'clock. No time to lose. By six he had cooked breakfast, given the dogs their feed, and packed the sled.

Pulling across the portage trail they finally reached the lower river, and on the ice the going was faster. In a short time Jim came in sight of the place where he had made a cache of his traps and fish bait. In the gray dawn light he could see a circling of black wings and hear a loud cawing and croaking. A dozen huge birds were tearing at the boughs that hid the fish. They were northern ravens—larger than crows and far more destructive to the small game of the woods.

Jim did not stop to shout. He brought up his rifle and fired into the middle of the flock, knocking down two of the black robbers. Their bodies he threw into the dog pail on the front of the toboggan. They were probably tough as leather, but the dogs would enjoy worrying them.

Fortunately the birds had succeeded in making off with only one or two of the precious fish. Jim loaded the rest on the sled with his traps, and gave the order to mush on.

All through the middle of the day he was setting his lower line. Some time after noon he got to the Beaver Lake portage and crossed over, baiting up traps around the lake. With a scant two hours of daylight left, he decided to push on over the trail to Porcupine River and get that section of the trap-line set up. It was a hard task but he went about it with a will. Five miles of overland trail, with perhaps a dozen traps to put in order—then five miles back, if he wanted to sleep at the Beaver Lake camp.

He trotted the dogs between cubbies and raced to each trap to work with quick, skilful hands. Even so it was after sunset when he sighted the winding thread of Porcupine River through the trees. In the fading afterglow, he swung the tired team and set a fast pace on the back trail. It grew dark early, there in the thick bush. A mile from the lake, Jim found he could no longer see the trail, and fell back to let Bruno's nose do the guiding. The big dog plodded steadily ahead. He knew what he had to do as well as if Jim had been able to tell him. Once a wolf howled far away to the north, and Pat paused, whimpering, but the lead dog jerked him on. They crossed the mile-wide stretch of open ice and pulled up panting in front of the log hut.

There were no kennels here, but Jim gave the faithful animals a good feed and bedded them down in the lee of the cabin wall. Ten minutes later both of them were curled up contentedly, with their tails sheltering their noses.

When he woke next morning, the boy found his own legs stiff from the long day's going. He wondered, while he dressed, what shape the dogs would be in. They had done no work for five months and he had given them a pretty stiff dose of trail yesterday—thirty miles of it. To his relief, both Pat and Bruno gave him a vociferous welcome. They were barking and jumping to the limit of their chains, as eager as a pair of yearling pups.

When the sled was loaded and the dogs harnessed, Jim led the way northward to the Squaw. There were eight or nine miles of trap-line to tend between Beaver Lake and his lower camp. He took his time, working methodically down river and enjoying the glint of early sun on the frost-rimed trees. Four ermine made up the morning's catch.

He found some repairs were needed at the lower cabin, and his supply of firewood had to be replenished. Chaining up the dogs, he spent the two or three hours of daylight that remained in making the log house snug and stacking up a sizable pile of wood. One of the dead trees he cut was on the river bank, fifty or sixty yards downstream from the camp. While he was chopping it, he noticed a line of tracks a short distance below and, going to investigate, he found that a pack of wolves had passed that way. The trail was fresh—not more than two hours old, he judged, and there had been at least four full-grown timber wolves in the band.

That night when he fed the dogs he found them silent but restless. Their ears were pricked up, listening to noises too faint for a human to catch. And hungry as he was, Bruno turned from his food once or twice to sniff the east wind uneasily. Jim knew the signs. He built a good fire in front of the camp and put on a couple of heavy logs that would last till morning.

If the wolves came by in the night they kept far enough away so that Jim's sleep was undisturbed. He hitched up his team in the morning, put bait and a dozen traps on the sled and pushed on down the river. There was good fur country for several miles beyond his lower camp and he meant to get the most out of it.

New cubbies had to be built along this outlying line. It was past noon when he came out at the edge of a burned-over tract that extended as far as he could see, down the Squaw. A blanket of brush had sprung up among the stark, dead poles of the burned spruces, but there was not enough cover to make good trapping country. Jim was just on the point of turning back, when a growl from Bruno drew his attention to a deer track in the snow near the bank.

He knelt and looked more closely. The crystals were still breaking and falling from the sides of the prints. Less than an hour old—probably only a few minutes. Jim looked up across the tree tops where the deer had entered the bush and saw a flock of ravens circling. He took his rifle out of its buckskin case and called to the dogs. "Come on—mush!" he said.

Leading the way up the bank, he broke a zigzag trail through the brush, following the slim, pointed tracks. It was hard going, with the sled. After a quarter of an hour they were close enough to see the ravens swooping low over something in the thicket, and Jim threw off the catch of his rifle. The dogs were trembling with excitement. The hair rose in stiff ridges on their shoulders, yet they made no sound. That meant wolves. Jim stepped forward as quietly as he could and caught a half glimpse of gray fur, scuttling off through the brush. The ravens settled to their feast with a raucous croaking.

In half a dozen more strides, the boy came on a dead buck lying in a red-stained patch of snow. The black scavengers rose on heavy wings at his approach and flew off, cawing angrily. He looked around. The deer had been hamstrung and rendered helpless before the wolves had torn out its throat. It was barely dead, its eyes just beginning to glaze, its body still warm.

Jim cut into the carcass and put the two hind quarters on his toboggan. "No use leaving good meat for wolves an' ravens," he told the dogs. "We'll eat well for a few days."

Before he left, he examined the wolf tracks around the body. Three or four different prints could be distinguished—probably the same pack that had crossed below his camp. They were all ordinary tracks, slightly larger than those made by a husky dog, but nothing to compare with the giant paw marks of the big lone wolf. Jim took a No. 4 trap off the sled and set it with care in the snow under the buck's shoulder. The chain was fastened to a huge clog, six inches through and eight feet long. He was just about to sprinkle the pan and jaws lightly with snow when he felt a soft chill on his face. The morning had been gray and overcast. Now big, slow flakes were beginning to fall. They would cover the trap far better than Jim could hope to do.

He led the dogs back to the river and headed up into the white swirl of the storm. It had grown colder and he was glad to pull up the hood of his parka, to protect his cheeks from the bite of the wind.

The snow did not fall very long. By the time they had reached the lower camp again there were breaks in the clouds overhead, and as soon as it grew dark the sky was filled with stars.

Jim and the dogs dined royally on venison that night. The cold snapped and crackled in the forest, but log walls shut it out. They slept soundly and woke to a still, glistening morning of bitterly low temperature. The first moment Jim stepped outside, he felt the breath catch in his nostrils. Forty below, it must be— at the least.

Up to the northwest, between the Squaw and the Esskagannega, there were some inland brooks that Jim had thought worth looking over. He put what traps he had left on the toboggan and set out soon after sunrise. Almost the first thing he saw, as he walked up the river ahead of his team, was a long gray animal followed by two smaller ones, moving along on the snow-covered ice. It was a mother otter and her two pups. She started running as soon as she caught the man-scent, and the young ones raced after her at a clumsy gait between a slide and a gallop.

Jim cut into the woods at the head of the next bend, taking a line to the north through the thick bush. Four or five inches had been added to the depth of snow in yesterday's storm, but still he found the breaking only moderately bad. Inside of an hour he reached the first brook and was delighted to find the banks covered with fresh mink sign. He began building trap-houses, and making water-sets in places where the current was too swift to freeze. The water-set for mink is a rather complicated affair but highly effective if properly done. With his ax, Jim cut a dozen alder switches and thrust them into the bed of the stream in a fencelike row close to the bank. Half a whitefish, with an alder stick run through it, was fastened to the fence. And just in front of it, on the shallow bottom, he placed a pair of No. 1 traps, their springs turned inward, toward the bait.

At another point in the stream he put his fence right across the current, arching it in a curve to withstand the rush of water. And still another set was made in the bottom of a bank tunnel, with the bait hanging above it.

By one o'clock Jim had completed a short trap-line along two of the brooks and swung his team toward home. He hoped, if there was still time, to make the run down river and look at his wolf trap. Tomorrow he would have to start westward again. Two hours of daylight remained when he reached the river, and without stopping at camp he urged the dogs down the well-beaten trail. A mounting excitement filled him, with each mile they covered. He had a hunch—a feeling of practical certainty—that the wolves had returned to their kill in the night.

A dozen paces ahead of the team, he plowed his way through the brush along the edge of the burnt land. There it was—the carcass of the buck—and beside it something dark in the trap. He ran closer, gripping his rifle. Then a groan of disgust escaped him. Every shred of meat was eaten off the deer's skeleton. The snow for yards around was trampled with wolf tracks. But all that the trap held was a dead raven, cut nearly in two by the heavy jaws. The bird must have come back first and sprung the trap. After that the gray killers had returned to feast in safety.

Jim took up the trap. It was no use resetting it, for the wolves had finished their meal. Throwing it on the sled, he started to plod the five miles back to camp.

Tired and disappointed as he was, the boy began to recover his spirits after half an hour of steady hiking. He laughed at himself for feeling sore at the unfortunate raven. After all, you had to expect days when things went wrong. It all evened up in the end. He tried whistling, but the folds of the parka muffled the sound and his stiff lips refused to pucker properly. Then he turned to thoughts of a good supper. In his supplies for the lower camp he had brought along a couple of jars of his mother's blueberry preserves. How about a blueberry pudding to give the day a happy ending? His mouth watered at the idea and his steps quickened unconsciously.

It was late when he got back to the cabin, and almost dark by the time he had a fire roaring in the stove. But he knew just where to lay his hands on that jar of berries. Scooping out a liberal quantity he mixed the sticky stuff into a batch of dough and thrust it in the stovepipe oven. Then he went about preparing the rest of the meal. Frozen mashed potatoes were dug out of the can with a knife and put in a pan to fry, along with a thick slab of venison steak. Meanwhile he warmed up the dog mash and took it out to the hungry team.

There was a queer sort of tang in the steamy air when he re-entered the cabin. He sniffed once or twice, trying to identify the smell, but his venison needed turning at the moment and he forgot all about it.

Soon the first course was ready. He filled a plate with the hot food and ate heartily. Now for the crowning glory of the meal—the blueberry pudding. That strange, sharp odor assailed his nostrils again as he approached the oven, but still he couldn't place it. The pudding was done to a turn—golden brown and tempting. He put a big slice of it in a bowl, then went to his precious store of evaporated milk and opened a tin for the occasion. Recklessly he poured nearly half a can of it, rich and creamy, over the hot pudding. With the relish of a gourmet he lifted the first mouthful to his lips—and suddenly dropped the spoon.

Vinegar! The truth dawned on him slowly. By the flickering glow of the candle he had lighted too late, he looked more closely at the jar of preserves. Instead of blueberries, he had made his dessert with pickled beets!

Well, all that good canned milk couldn't be wasted.

TRAP-LINES NORTH

He tried the pudding again and decided it wasn't so
bad when you got used to it. Grimly he ate it, to the
last spoonful. Then his sense of humor got the best of
him, and he lay back roaring with laughter till the
cabin shook and the dogs answered from their kennels.
The end of a perfect day!

X

Jim started the return trip to his home camp in the morning. With a stop at each trap along the line it was impossible to make much speed, but he covered the seventeen miles to the cabin at Long Portage before nightfall. A single ermine was all he found in the traps —not a very profitable day's work. It was not quite so cold that night, and he slept comfortably in the lean-to, with a good fire in front of the entrance.

Four or five hours of travel the next day brought him in sight of the upper camp. The slant sunlight of afternoon fell gently on the snowy roof, but Jim's ears told him that all was not as peaceful as it looked. There was a great squalling of jays and chattering of squirrels from the sheltered side of the cabin where he had his moose meat hung.

He shoveled the snow away from the door with a snowshoe, ran inside and got his shotgun. When he came around the corner of the camp the battle was still in progress. Four or five red squirrels were tearing at the frozen meat, while a flock of gorbies squawked and fluttered, trying to drive them away. Jim lifted the gun and fired both barrels in quick succession. The hail of shot cut through the middle of the mêlée scattering the combatants in all directions. As the echoes of the double report died away, a sudden silence fell. Jim picked up the bodies of half a dozen jays and two squirrels and tossed them to the dogs. Then he went to examine the meat. In spite of the fact that it was frozen to rocklike hardness, the thieves had destroyed almost two-thirds of the flesh.

The boy looked at it with glum discouragement. Losing provisions was a serious matter back here in the bush. He had counted on that quarter of meat to last him through till Christmas. And thinking of Christmas he wondered just how long it would be before the holiday. In the cabin he had a stick with notches cut for days. Now he went in and with the help of his diary tried to bring the calendar up to date. As nearly as he could figure this was the 23rd of November. When he saw Lindsay he would be able to check up.

Turning to the preparation of supper, Jim found another minor calamity had come to his food supply. Some small animal had crawled in through a chink in the logs and gnawed a hole in the grub box. More than a cupful of flour was scattered on the dirt floor. Wood mice must have done the damage. He plugged the hole as best he could with a peg of hardwood, and found a big tin can in which to place the flour bag. The life of a trapper, he told himself sadly, was not all roses.

A gray light was beginning to steal into the cabin next morning when Jim roused and peered over the edge of his eiderdown. Something besides the light had wakened him—a sound like a tiny, high-pitched shriek. He rubbed the sleep out of his eyes and looked across the floor to the opposite corner of the hut. There was a slender bit of white fur over there in the semidarkness, and two beady black eyes staring at him. A weasel!

Jim lifted himself slowly and carefully on one elbow. As his vision cleared he could see a small body under the weasel's fore paws. "Good boy!" breathed the youngster with a grin. "Fixed that low-down mouse that ate my flour, didn't you?"

He sat perfectly still and watched. After a few seconds the ermine sank its teeth in its victim's throat, drank the blood, then turned and vanished silently. There was a savage efficiency in its technique that made the boy shiver. He remembered a saying of his father's —that if weasels were as big as coyotes, no man would ever be safe in the woods. Yet he couldn't help admiring the sheer, ferocious daring of the tiny killer.

When he had dressed and built the fire, he spent ten minutes hunting for the hole by which the weasel and

its prey had entered. Apparently the walls were solid.
At last he gave up the search and got breakfast.

There were plenty of chores to occupy Jim around
the camp that day. He melted a big bucketful of snow
water and washed his clothes, hanging them to dry
on the rack above the stove. Then he put a batch of
bread in the oven to bake, and went out with his ax to
get in a supply of wood.

About noon he was dragging a long butt log back
to the cabin, when the dogs set up a furious barking.
Looking out on the river he saw a short, squat figure
breaking trail for three gaunt huskies and a battered
old toboggan. The man was coming down from the
direction of Squaw Lake, slogging along with bent
knees, his mittened hands hanging low. At Jim's trail he
paused and swung in toward the camp.

Jim dropped his log by the woodpile and went down
the bank to meet his visitor. It was the Cree Indian,
Joe Leake.

The man pulled off his snowshoes and thrust them,
toes up, into the snow in front of the lead dog. It was
equivalent to an order to the team to stay where they
were. Then he raised a hand in silent greeting and came
up the path.

"How are you, Joe?" asked Jim. He had no tobacco
to offer his guest, so he went into the cabin and took the
kettle of hot water off the stove. Sprinkling a little tea

in a pan he set it to brew and motioned the Indian to a seat on the bench. As soon as the tea was ready he poured it into a tin cup and placed it on the table with a can of sugar.

Joe Leake measured out half a teaspoonful of the precious sweetening and stirred the tea vigorously. When he had gulped down a swallow or two, he offered the cup to Jim.

"You ketchum fur—plenty good, eh?" he inquired politely.

"Fair," said Jim. "Nothing special, yet. How are you making out?"

"Plenty fisher," the Indian replied. "Nobody ketchum fisher like Joe Leake."

There were no more remarks for a time. The Cree sipped noisily at the tea. When it was gone he stood up and reached a hand into his breeches pocket. It came out holding a dirty stub of lead pencil.

"Boy take-um," Joe Leake explained. "Me bringum back."

He laid the pencil carefully on the table and walked out.

"Well, I'll be—" Jim murmured under his breath. "Say Joe, thanks a heap. I sure do appreciate it."

He went after him down the trail and saw him stoop by the sled to pull back the canvas cover. Out came a pair of new moose-hide moccasins. The Indian said nothing but pushed them into Jim's hands. Then he

slipped his feet into the snowshoe straps, barked a guttural command to the dogs and led his team away, up
river.

The boy was so surprised he could scarcely shout his
thanks after the departing sled. When the Indian was
out of sight he carried the moccasins into the cabin,
admiring their skilful workmanship. Then he went
back to his wood chopping. Every time he thought of
the Cree's thirty-mile journey to return a two-inch bit
of pencil he shook his head and chuckled. It was typical
of the scrupulous honesty that made all white men of
the North respect a woods Indian. And yet he had
read in books and heard tenderfoot sportsmen remark
that the redskin was no better than a thieving crook!

The gift of moccasins was Leake's way of expressing
his gratitude for the dose of medicine they had given
the boy. Without being told, Jim knew his mother
must have received some similar present.

By bedtime his clothes on the frame over the stove
were well dried. The bread he had baked came out of
the oven crisp and brown. In the morning he would
be ready to take the trail again.

Bruno and Pat were thoroughly rested and eager to
be off when he buckled on their harness, shortly after
sunrise. They mushed across country to Whitefish Lake
and followed the trap-line around its shores. A mile or
so beyond, on the trail to Porcupine Lake, Jim had a
No. 3 trap set in a fox path. It was a hundred yards

from the main track, so he left the dogs, took his rifle
and went in alone. As he neared the place he saw something move beyond a low thicket. A great round head
with tufted ears and glaring yellow eyes lifted to stare
at him. "Lynx!" he thought instantly, and leveled the
rifle.

But in the second when his front sight came on the
head, he knew it wasn't a lynx. The yellow eyes blinked
at him solemnly and instead of a snarling cat nose he
saw a short, hooked beak. The trap held a horned owl!

Jim killed the bird and spread it out on the snow. It
was the first time he had seen one of its species so close.
The body, from ear tufts to tail, was nearly two feet
long, and the wings spanned between five and six feet.
He began to understand, when he saw its huge, feathered talons, how these big owls could wreak such havoc
among the smaller woods animals.

There was no fur in the traps around Porcupine
Lake, and by the time Jim had tended them all it was
too late to go farther that afternoon. He made himself and the dogs comfortable at the lean-to on the
west shore and spent the night there.

The next two days were uneventful. They traveled
down Porcupine River to the camp Jim had built and
explored the country below for several miles. It was
low, desolate ground without much sign of game or
fur. Dead trees rose gray and bearded out of the endless
muskeg. A few otter trails were visible along the stream

courses, but the boy saw only one mink track and no fisher. The sky clouded over and the air grew heavy. It felt like a storm.

A few inches of snow fell in the night and the morning broke cold and clear. Jim was glad to turn his back on the barren muskeg and break trail up the river again. In the traps below Porcupine Lake he found two snowshoe rabbits—worthless as fur, but a welcome change of diet for the dogs. They ate them, hide and all.

"That'll grow you a warm coat," Jim told Bruno. He was convinced, as all northern trappers are, that rabbit fur makes a dog's hair come in thicker.

The last trap he visited that night held a prize that made up for many fruitless days. It was a slim black fisher. A female—smaller but more valuable than any male because of her finer fur. Jim gloated over the lustrous sheen of the dark pelt, and took exceptional pains with the skinning.

Next morning he led the team across the clean white expanse of the lake and struck overland to a chain of small ponds that lay to the east. High, dry poplar ridges made it a pleasant country. Good fur country too, if the maze of rabbit tracks meant anything. He built half a dozen cubbies and set traps in them before returning to the lean-to at sunset. The following day would be the last of November if his reckoning was right. Two weeks since he had seen a white man. A homesickness for human companionship took hold of him and he decided he would start up to meet Lindsay in the morning.

In his eagerness he woke while the night was still pitch black, made a quick breakfast and routed out the dogs. He might have to go all the way to the head of Squaw Lake before he encountered his brother, and this time of year there was only a scant six hours of daylight. Then he started packing the sled and realized with some disappointment that he would have to go back to his home camp first. The fisher skin was not yet dry and the dog pail was empty of meal. Grumbling, he headed the team northward. Even the two ermine and the mink that he found in his traps along the line were scant recompense for the loss of a day.

It was nearing noon when they drew close to the Squaw. Old Bruno lifted his nose, gave a joyful whine and flung his weight into the collar. There was a sharp, inquiring bark from across the river, answered at once by staccato yelps from Jim's team. Smoke was coming from the cabin stovepipe.

Lumbering into a run, the boy crossed the ice ahead of the dogs and climbed the bank with a whoop. Lindsay's blond head appeared suddenly in the doorway.

"Hi!" grinned the younger brother. "Where've you been? I came down last night, wanting to visit a little. Nobody here so I made myself at home."

"It's a lucky thing I had this fisher skin," Jim

laughed. "If it hadn't been for bringing it back here I'd be mushing up Squaw Lake by now. Got a sort of hankering to see you last night. Gosh knows why! How've you been doing, you old stick-in-the-mud?"

They chained the dogs and went into the warm cabin. Lindsay had a pan of hash sizzling on the stove and was preparing to make cocoa.

"Nothing like being free with the supplies when you're in another man's camp," he chuckled. "Come up my way some time an' I'll pay you back."

It was good to sprawl by the stove and chat steadily while they ate. Each tried to recount every happening of the past two weeks, and they talked till their throats were sore from unaccustomed use.

"We sound like a couple o' gorbies," Jim grinned at length. "But it sure is fun to have somebody to gab to. Let's play cards. Did you bring that old pack along?"

Lindsay went to get the playing cards out of his possible-sack and paused as he reached the dark corner of the room.

"Say," he remarked, pointing to the floor, "what's the idea of laying out your meat like this?"

"Meat?" Jim asked, puzzled. "What meat?"

"Mice—three of 'em," laughed Lindsay. "Don't tell me you didn't put 'em here!"

The older boy went over to join him. "Well I'm a son of a gun!" he murmured. The small bodies lay in a neat row between the grub box and the wall, each with a red puncture in its throat.

Jim scratched his head. "I guess that weasel must have adopted me," he grinned. "Better'n a watchdog, any day. And he sure has been working overtime since I left!"

XI

THAT night as they lay in their sleeping-bags Lindsay made a suggestion. "You've just been over your line," he told Jim. "How about taking a few days off and making a trip up to my country? There ought to be foxes on that long bay south of Squaw Lake, but I've never tried any blind sets. You could show me how."

Jim liked the idea. "We'll go tomorrow," he said, "and work together a while. I don't need to start down over my line for another week."

It was only about seven miles up the Squaw to Lindsay's lower camp, and the boys arrived shortly before noon. Without stopping for lunch they pushed the two teams on into the bay that made a deep indentation in the southern shore line of the lake.

As Lindsay had prophesied, the snow along the banks

was dotted thickly with foxes tracks. Jim studied the lay of the land a while and nodded.

"You're right," he said. "It's a good place for blind sets. Have you got any No. 4 traps along?"

"Four of 'em," the younger brother replied. "Right here on the sled."

"Okay," said Jim. "Go over there to the edge of the lake and pull a couple of armfuls of long grass."

While Lindsay was gone, he chopped up a frozen fish into small bits and scraped a place clear of snow in one of the fox paths. On the bare ground he spread the fish over an area about a foot square. Then he fastened the trap chain to a stake, which he drove solidly into the frozen earth with his ax.

"Now look," he told his brother. "I'm going to set the trap and put it right on top of the fish. Then I take the grass and spread it out like this, not too thick, but thick enough to hide the trap. Sprinkle a little wet snow over it and it'll freeze into a sort of mat. There— that's all there is to a blind set."

They went on and placed the other three big traps at strategic points around the bay. By dusk they were back at Lindsay's cabin, ready for supper. It had been cloudy all afternoon and now it was snowing a little.

"The wind's changing," said Jim, sniffing the air before bedtime. "This won't be much of a storm."

In the morning the air was clear and only an inch or

two of snow had been added to the winter's white blanket.

"A good day for tracking," Lindsay offered. "Let's take a swing up around Sucker Lake. I haven't been to look at those traps for more than a week."

"By the way, what date is this?" Jim asked. "Near as I can figure, it's the second of December, but I may have dropped a day, somewhere along."

Lindsay looked at his precious calendar. "Gee, I don't know," he frowned. "Seems to me it ought to be the first—or the thirtieth of November. I marked off the days at the beginning, but after my first trip around the line I sort of forgot about it."

Jim let out a roar. "That's what comes of being fancy in the bush!" he laughed. "You're worse off than I am. At least I know what month it is!"

They took the trail north to Sucker Lake after breakfast. The early sun slanted through the forest, its level rays gilding the spruce boles. Chickadees chirped gaily. Swinging along over the snow, with their breath rising in white clouds, the boys joked and skylarked as they went.

"Have to show you how it's done in a real trapping country," Lindsay bragged. "Bet I catch some fur this morning. I feel it in my bones."

Jim grinned and pointed ahead to the first cubby. "Yep. I reckon you're right," he said. "Looks like something in the trap."

The younger boy ran forward eagerly and bent over the trap-house.

"Aw, shucks!" Jim heard him say. When he straightened up his face was red and sheepish. In his hand was the draggled form of a whisky-jack.

"Was it fur you felt in your bones," asked Jim innocently, "or feathers?"

Lindsay was too disgusted to reply to this thrust. He stalked ahead in silence, while Jim whistled cheerfully behind him. A quarter of a mile beyond, there was a fork in the trail.

"You take this one ahead," Lindsay said briefly. "I've got a No. 4 set over that way."

Jim went on, breaking trail for the two teams, and a few steps brought him to a neatly built cubby. The trap was sprung. Twenty feet away he found it, where the clog had snagged in a thicket, and in the jaws was the frozen body of a mink.

Jim chuckled as he took it out and started back to the sleds. At that moment a yell of triumph came echoing through the woods.

"Hey!" Lindsay was shouting. "Bring the rifle. I got a brush wolf!"

The dogs were sniffing the air and growling. "Shut up, you, Bruno!" Jim ordered. "And stay here!" He grabbed up the .32 from his toboggan and ran back to the place where his brother had turned off. Two minutes later he saw the boy, club in hand, circling warily around a big coyote, caught by the forepaw.

The wolf was crouched, his teeth bared. At the sight of a new enemy he made a desperate lunge, and jerked the trap and its heavy clog several yards into the cover of a clump of small jack-pines.

"Hold still," Jim called. "I can see enough of him for a shot."

He aimed at a patch of yellow-gray fur just behind the left shoulder, and squeezed the trigger. At the crack of the rifle, the coyote gave a convulsive bound and fell in a twitching heap.

"Wait!" Jim warned, but Lindsay had kicked off his snowshoes and run into the thicket, brandishing his club. There was a sudden stir and a grating, gasping snarl that ended in the metallic chop of teeth. Lindsay came tumbling backward out of the brush.

"Whew!" he breathed as he picked himself up. "Son of a gun! He tore my pants!"

There was a clean slash in one knee of his mackinaw-cloth breeches, but the teeth had not broken the skin.

"Reckon he moved," said Jim. "I must have got him in the lung instead of the heart." He jerked another cartridge into the breech and drilled the wolf cleanly through the head.

Lindsay got his feet on the long springs of the trap and held them down while the older boy pulled the coyote's paw free. Jim caught the animal by the hind legs and swung it over his shoulder.

"He's a big one, all right," he said. "Heavy. Must weigh close to forty pounds. They don't get lean in a good rabbit year."

They put the dead wolf on Lindsay's sled and went on up the trap-line. The sight of the mink had filled the younger brother with glee. "Didn't I tell you?" he rubbed it in. "You're in real fur country now, my boy!"

After a night in the camp on Sucker Lake they traveled on to the head of Squaw, tending the traps as they went. Progress was slow that day, for Paddy, Jim's big mongrel second dog, had cut his paw on the edge of an ax. The wound was not very deep but it bled a good deal. Luckily there was an old shirt in the cabin which Lindsay had discarded on a previous trip, and with it they were able to bandage the foot.

Along the route to Poplar Lake and Lindsay's home camp, the following day, they found no fur except an ermine or two. When they got to the cabin, Pat was limping along on three legs, a very tired dog. It was obvious that he would have to rest if his paw were to heal properly.

They spent a day there, working out several short trap-lines which Lindsay had set near his camp.

Next morning the boys decided to leave Jim's sled, hitch up the three sound dogs, and let the invalid ride on the toboggan.

[120]

This plan was not put into execution without some difficulty. First of all, Lindsay's lead dog resented being put into second place. No sooner were they in harness than he launched a growling attack on Bruno, and the veteran police dog was in the process of giving him a sound thrashing when the boys beat them apart. Then poor old Paddy, unused to luxury, scrambled off the sled as soon as they started, and limped ahead, trying to take his place in the traces. Only when Jim walked beside the toboggan and talked to him reassuringly for a mile or more, did he submit to being a passenger.

That day—the 6th of December as Jim reckoned it —they went up Cranberry River as far as the foot of Cordingley Lake. It was the nearest either of them had been to civilization since their trip to Nakina to get the family. Lindsay had a few traps along the river but they found nothing in them.

At noon they were about to turn back when a moving speck appeared on the ice, far up by Pointed Rock.

"Might be somebody we know from town," said Lindsay. "You stay here with the dogs an' I'll go meet him."

It was a clear day, not too cold for comfort, and Jim sat down on the tarpaulin that covered the loaded sled. He watch the two specks approach each other till they met, half a mile away. For a minute or two they stood there talking. Then Lindsay turned back, waved an arm in farewell and came down the white lake surface at a trot.

"Say—what do you think!" he panted as he drew near. "That was Michel Lagarde. He says Dad came back day before yesterday. He's at Waba now!"

"Gosh!" Jim beamed. "How is he? Did Michel say?"

"Awful thin, he told me, but tickled to be home an' cracking jokes with everybody at the station," Lindsay replied. "How quick could we get over there? I'm ready to start this minute!"

"We'll have to go back for my sled," said Jim. "Then you can go right across tomorrow. I'll be slower, with Pat, but I'll come as soon as I can make it back to my camp."

At dawn next morning, Lindsay waved good-by and led his team out of the cove, headed eastward toward Wababimiga. Jim envied him. He would have given a prime mink skin to see his father before nightfall, as the younger boy would. However, he had been away from his home camp a week, and the injured dog had to be considered.

Two days of rest had done wonders for the big mongrel's paw. Jim put on a fresh bandage, harnessed the team, and started north half an hour after his brother's departure. The dog pulled willingly, his limp hardly perceptible. They stopped for a rest at midday, then went on at an easy pace down the long, white highway of Squaw Lake. Darkness overtook them just as they reached Lindsay's lower camp.

The short trip from there to Jim's main cabin was completed by noon the following day. The boy built up his fire at once, washed some clothes, and put a pan of bread in the oven. While it baked he left the dogs to rest and visited some of his nearby traps. All but one was empty. In that he found the bones of a rabbit and a few shreds of fur, left by the ravens.

There was better luck awaiting him on the trail to Wababimiga next morning. In quick succession he took a mink and two ermine from the traps near Whitefish Pond. And three miles farther on, just as he came in sight of Porcupine Lake, he found the frozen body of a cross-fox. It was his first of the season and a real catch—worth two or three times as much as a common red fox pelt. The long, soft hair was tawny underneath, shading into gray along the back, and marked with the black, cross-shaped patch on the shoulders.

Jim had barely had time to put the fox on his toboggan and tie up the cover fastenings, when he saw something moving out on the lake ahead. It was a small herd of caribou, drifting like gray smoke across the snowy surface. Behind them trotted a single gray speck. The distance was almost half a mile, and at first glance Jim thought it was a caribou calf that had fallen behind the herd, but as he pushed through the trees for a clearer view, he muttered an exclamation. The lone follower was a timber wolf.

Quickly the boy raised his rifle and steadied it in a tree crotch. It was a long shot—almost an impossible shot—but he was resolved to try it anyway. He allowed for a light wind, blowing across from the south, lifted his sights to take care of the distance, and gently pressed the trigger. The crack of the rifle sounded startlingly loud in the stillness. For the space of a heart-beat nothing happened. Then a tiny white cloud appeared for an instant right at the wolf's side. The animal leaped upward like a jack-in-the-box, whirled in the air and landed running. Jim held the rifle ready for a second shot, but the wolf offered a poor target. He was moving fast and straight away toward the woods on the opposite shore. His long bounds threw up the snow behind him in white spurts like puffs of smoke. If the bullet had found him at all it had certainly done no damage to his speed.

The boy trudged back to the restless dogs. "Well," he told them, "it was a pretty fair shot, at that. Couldn't have missed him by more'n a foot. Say—" he continued, musing to himself, "I wonder if he was the old big one. All alone like that—come on, you, Bruno —mush!"

They crossed the trail of the caribou band a few minutes later, and Jim stopped to make a careful search in the packed snow. But the wolf had been traveling in the path beaten by the broad splay hoofs of the deer, and had left no recognizable sign.

[124]

The brief winter daylight was beginning to wane already, and there were still seven or eight miles of unbroken trail to cover before night. However, Jim was beyond the trap-line now, and he pushed along steadily, the dogs close to his heels. Once he felt an extra weight when he lifted his feet and knew that Bruno was saving work by walking on the snowshoe tails. It was a trick the old lead dog had learned years before, in deep, soft snow, but today the going was comparatively easy. At a sharp word from his master the dog dropped back, a comically guilty look on his wise gray face.

As dusk fell, they came down out of the high bush, crossed the eastern arm of Wababimiga and rounded a point into the home cove. A light glowed yellow in the cabin window. Jim let out a high-pitched whoop and broke into a run on the beaten lake trail. Yelping with joy the dogs galloped behind him. And as they came up the path Jim saw a great, gaunt figure, silhouetted in the open door.

"Hi, boy!" came the strong voice of his father.

Fisher

XII

BIG LINDSAY VANDERBECK was still far from the mighty man he had once been. Even prepared as Jim was, he felt a shock of dismay at his father's thinness and the pallor under his seamed, weatherbeaten skin. But inwardly he was unchanged. There was courage in his twinkling gray eyes as he joked about his own feebleness.

"What do you think I raised you big galoots for?" he asked. "Just so I could sit around in my old age an' be comfortable, that's all. This is goin' to be good practice for me. I ain't ever had a chance to watch other folks work till now, an' it certainly is a handsome sight!"

Wrapped up in plenty of warm clothes he was sitting on the big chopping block back of the cabin, while Jim and Lindsay sawed firewood.

He listened with eager interest to the boys' accounts of their trapping. "That sounds like a pretty fair catch o' fur," he commented. "But you youngsters'll have to step lively to keep ahead o' me, when I get goin' again. I aim to set up all the south shore o' the lake an' along those brooks that run into the Waba River. The girls have got a nice little line workin' already. Take a look at that fur in the shed. Must be a hundred dollars' worth, I should think. Maybe more, if prices are good."

Jim threw a fresh log into the crotch of the sawhorse and paused to stretch his arms. "Tell you what, Dad," he said. "Lindsay an' I can make a start on that line down the brooks while we're here. Then you'll be all ready to tend the traps in a week or so."

"I don't want to keep you away from your ground too long," his father answered. "But if you could take time for that it would be a big help, sure enough."

The boys set out with one sled next morning, and put in two days building cubbies and setting traps, over to the eastward. Big Lindsay had built a small cabin on one of the streams, and they spent the nights there. As they were returning to Wababimiga, the morning of December 13, they saw fresh snowshoe tracks leading off the trail. The prints were unblurred and distinct. Lindsay knelt for a moment, examining them and beckoned to Jim.

"Come on," he said. "It's Ida. See that place in the toe of the right shoe? I patched that for her the day I got here. She's in there tending a trap. Let's go meet her."

They had followed the trail a few hundred yards when they heard their sister's voice from the other side of a thicket.

"Oh, you beauty!" she was exclaiming. "How'm I going to get you out? You're a lot too pretty to kill!"

"Hey—what you got?" called the younger boy, running nearer.

As they came around the thicket they saw a slim black animal caught in the trap. Its back was arched like an angry cat's, and it crouched facing its enemies with white teeth bared.

"A fisher!" cried Jim. "And say—isn't she a little honey! Maybe we can take her alive, Ida. Let me have that gunny sack and I'll try it."

He stepped slowly closer to the trapped animal, holding open the mouth of the empty bag. When he was near enough he flipped it over the fisher's head and body and pressed it tightly into the snow, while his prisoner thrashed and whirled inside.

"Open the trap quick, Lindsay," he ordered, "before she hurts that leg."

It took his brother only a few seconds to push down the spring and pry open the steel jaws. As the pressure was released, the fisher jerked her paw free, and Jim picked her up in the bag.

"There!" he cried in triumph. "We'll fix up a cage, back at camp, and you can keep her for a pet."

When they reached the cabin and displayed their prize, there were exclamations of delight from Mary and her mother.

"You poor, scared little thing!" said Mrs. Vanderbeck consolingly. "You're going to be taken care of now—don't you fret. Boys—get busy right off, an' build some sort of a pen for her. There's a roll of strong chicken wire in the shed."

By supper time they had put up four solid posts, braced at the top, and covered the cage with heavy, fine-meshed wire. In one corner was a little wooden hut with clean sawdust on the floor. When all was ready, Jim opened the sack and dropped the fisher gently inside the pen. She made a swift circuit of the wire, sniffed suspiciously at the hut, climbed up the mesh to investigate the top covering and finally retired to a corner where she cowered as far from her captors as possible.

Mrs. Vanderbeck came out with a piece of fish. "Go on away now, everybody," she said, "and let Miranda an' me get acquainted. I'm going to call her Miranda because she's such a handsome, dark thing. I read a book once about a black-haired girl called that, an' always thought it was a pretty name."

Next morning, after the breakfast dishes were out of the way and the cabin straightened up, Mrs. Vanderbeck went back to the fisher's pen. The rest of the family, standing at a respectful distance, watched her approach slowly toward the wire. She was holding a bit of frozen whitefish and talking in a low, friendly voice.

Miranda crouched in the snow outside her shelter. Her nose twitched and lifted toward the fish, but for several minutes she did not stir. Then with a quick movement she darted forward a foot or two. The woman waited, still speaking softly, and again the animal came nearer.

This was repeated several times, until Miranda stood on her hind legs, holding the side of the cage with her front paws and stretching upward eagerly toward the food. Only then did Mrs. Vanderbeck push it slowly through the mesh and let the fisher take it from her fingers.

"There now!" she beamed. "She's all over being scared. I think she'll make a real pet."

"Yes, but don't go an' get too fond of her," rumbled Big Lindsay with a grin. "Remember times are hard, an' that pelt's worth upwards of fifty dollars."

Jim had always known his mother had a "way" with animals. In other years they had kept foxes, bear cubs and even a full-grown lynx in contented captivity. In another pen, a short distance from Miranda's, a pair of sleek brown minks had their home.

All that day the boys' axes rang in the woods on a hill behind the camp. They hauled sledload after sledload of dry logs down to the cabin, and by nightfall there was a good two months' supply of firewood stacked up, ready for sawing. The girls would fit it for the stove as it was needed.

Mrs. Vanderbeck had been baking most of the day. When Jim and Lindsay packed their toboggans, the morning of the 15th, each had several loaves of fresh bread carefully wrapped against the cold.

"Ten more days to Christmas," their mother reminded them. "You'll have time to get over your lines, but don't lose track o' the calendar. We want to be all together again Christmas Eve."

She kissed each of them with a hearty smack, they shouted their farewells to the rest of the family, and the two teams trotted down the path to the cove.

"So long, kid," said Jim when they reached the point. "Good luck with the traps. I won't be getting up to your country before Christmas, but I'll see you here."

Their trails drew apart, Lindsay's leading straight up the lake to the west, Jim's swinging northeastward.

He waved a good-by to his brother, and led the dogs
into the bush, headed for Porcupine. It was a cold,
cloudy day with a hint of snow to come, but the boy's
spirits were high and the dogs, well rested, pulled
with a will. They made good time.

Only one incident broke the day's steady travel.
When they had gone a couple of miles overland from
Wababimiga, Jim, walking ahead, caught a glimpse
of something alive in the brush a little way off the
trail. At the same moment the dogs got the scent
and began to bark. He silenced them with a quick
command, stuck up his snowshoes in front of the
team to keep them from moving, and carried his rifle
ready as he went toward the thicket.

The animal had not moved again but he was sure
he could make out a blotch of cloudy gray fur between the spruce tips. As he rounded the edge of the
brush he halted in sheer astonishment. Squatting on
its haunches in a rabbit path sat a big lynx, staring
at him with unblinking yellow eyes. There was no
sign of trap or clog. Instinctively Jim had whipped
up his rifle, thinking the animal was fair game. Only
when he was looking down the sights did he realize
that the lynx was caught in a snare. Above it a slender
sapling bent in a curve, and from the tip of the tree
to the beast's neck ran a light, taut cord. It was common white string, hardly bigger than the twine used
in the store at Nakina. The lynx could have broken

[132]

it with a stroke of his paw, yet there he sat, afraid to move.

Jim had heard of this trait before. He knew that Indians sometimes caught the big cats in ordinary rabbit snares. Once the noose was around the throat, a lynx would stay put till it was found, or died of starvation.

"Well, old feller," he told the cat pityingly, "I can't do much for you, because I reckon you belong to Joe Leake. Still, there's no use letting you suffer."

He lifted the rifle again and sent a merciful bullet into the round, furry head.

The boy got back to his home camp at sundown, and began preparations for the morrow's trip down the Squaw. He had been living high during the four days at Waba. Now he would go back to the sparse fare of the trail. Aside from the two loaves of home-baked bread he put in his wangan there was only jerked moose meat, enough bacon to grease the frying pan, a little flour, tea, sugar and salt.

Waking before dawn next morning, he saw a gliding ribbon of white in the dark corner of the cabin. The weasel was back again, hunting mice around the grub chest. Jim sat up, chuckling.

"You little devil, you," he murmured, "it's time you had a name. From now on I'm going to call you Tiger. Tige for short. Are you hungry, Tige? Here!"

Beside him, on the table, there was a scrap of dry

moose meat. He tossed it into the corner and the
ermine crept toward it, its tiny nose sniffing suspiciously. A foot away it turned in disdain and glided
out of sight behind the grub box. What the little
killer wanted was fresh, hot blood.

It had snowed in the night but the day broke fair,
and Jim reached the long portage that afternoon. The
traps on the way down had yielded four ermine and
a mink besides a number of rabbits which he gave
to the dogs. Leaving the team in camp at the head
of the carry, he pushed on across, breaking trail.
It was just sunset when he came out on the river ice.
Across from him, on the opposite bank, the bushes
parted and a large buck deer stepped daintily forth.
Hardly more than fifty feet away, it paused to look
straight at him. Then, without a sign of fear, it trotted
quietly down river and into the woods again on the
nearer side.

"Guess you must keep track o' the calendar," Jim
remarked to the buck's vanishing tail flag. "Three
weeks ago you'd have been in season, and I bet I
couldn't have got within half a mile of you."

He turned back up the portage trail and reached
camp before dark. As soon as supper was finished and
he had skinned his fur, he crawled into the sleeping-
bag. Breaking trail for nine or ten hours on end was
tiring, even to long and powerful legs like Jim's.

Again he was up before dawn, making ready for

the next stretch of travel. The first two miles, over the path he had tramped the night before, was easy going. Then they struck the deep snow down the river and began plodding more slowly.

There was nothing in the first few traps the boy visited. He had begun to think his luck had left him, when a commotion in the snow ahead restored his hopes. Some sort of dark animal was floundering near one of the trap-houses, trying to drag the clog through an alder bush. Jim ran forward eagerly to get a closer view of his catch. It was smaller than a fox—smaller than a fisher—but its fur was a beautiful jet-black. Another few steps and he saw it had a stripe of white running down the back and along the full-furred tail.

"What in thunder—" he murmured in excitement. Here was a new kind of animal—something he had never seen in all his experience in the bush. He came within four or five yards, still wondering what such a rare pelt might be worth. Then suddenly he halted. A wave of strange, rank odor engulfed him. Coughing, half strangled, he backed off hastily. Even the dogs were cowering in the traces, sniffing and snorting their distaste.

At last Jim knew what he had in his trap. He had read stories about skunks. He drew a deep breath and held it, advancing with the rifle raised. His shot was hurried, but it took devastating effect, blowing the black-and-white beast almost to pieces. With relief the boy breathed again, and instantly regretted it. The nauseous fumes were thicker and more over-powering than ever. He stumbled back to the dogs and led them in a wide circuit, passing the place as far to the other side of the river as he could get. All that afternoon the scent hung around him, and even when he reached Beaver Lake that night he hung his outer clothing in a tree rather than sleep with it in the cabin.

Before Jim got into bed he wrote this entry in his little black notebook:

"Dec. 17. To Beaver Lake. Get one skunk, first I ever saw or caught. He is very foul. Alive. Shoot him. Smells worse. So I leave him, trap and all."

.Mink

XIII

At daylight Jim woke and built a fire, then crawled back into his eiderdown till the interior of the hut was warm. Still in his woolen underwear, he got breakfast. And finally, pulling on the Hudson Bay duffels over his heavy socks, he charged out into the sharp morning cold. The night's airing had done a good deal for his parka, sweater and blanket-cloth breeches. Back in the heated cabin they made him wrinkle his nose a little as he put them on, but their odor was no longer unbearable. The more he thought about his adventure the funnier it appeared to him. By the time he had the dogs harnessed he was laughing so hard the tears ran down his face and froze on his cheeks.

From Beaver Lake he cut back to the Squaw and followed the trap-line down river to his lower camp, which he reached in the middle of the day. He had intended to push on a few miles, but a glimpse of the cabin he caught from the river changed his plans. Something was wrong up there.

Scrambling up the bank ahead of the team he found the stout door of hewn planks hanging open on one hinge. A ridge of snow had drifted in across the threshold log, and the earthen floor beyond was littered with chips, scraps of paper and spilt flour.

Jim's scowl was black as he strode inside. A large hole had been gnawed in the grub box and all the provisions which were not in tin cans had been wholly or partially destroyed. Looking around more carefully he found the tracks of a porcupine and many squirrels in the snow around the entrance. But no squirrel or hedgehog alive could have played such havoc with the door.

The hinges had been double straps of thick moose hide, firmly nailed in place. He saw that the upper one was wrenched free, the nails pulled out of the solid spruce. It had taken weight and strength to do that. Rust on the nails showed that the damage had been done some time before, and several snows had fallen in the meantime, obliterating any tracks that might have shown outside.

TRAP-LINES NORTH

It was while he was putting the door back in place that Jim came on the sole clue he was ever to find in this mystery. Caught behind a splinter on the outer surface of one of the planks was a long, stiff hair, gray-white at one end, shading to dark brown at the other. The boy had scraped enough moose skins to recognize it instantly. Perhaps some big bull had thought the cabin was an enemy. Perhaps he had merely rubbed his huge body a little too hard against the door. At any rate, a moose had begun the trouble that the rodents had finished.

He nailed the hinge fast with his ax and set about tidying up the floor. By the time he had made things shipshape it was too near dark to go any farther. He cooked supper, fed the dogs and got ready for bed.

He still had traps to visit down river as far as the burnt land. Breaking trail, next morning, he was striding along, a dozen paces ahead of the dogs, when he heard an ominous crackle under his feet. The next instant he was plunging downward through the ice. In that second while he fell, a chain of swift thoughts flashed through his mind. Water—freezing cold— would he be able to get out—or to build a fire if he did?

But amazingly there was no water. He landed with a crash on solid ice five feet down. A rocky rapid just below had dammed up the river before the big

[139]

freeze came in November. When the water went down it had left a shell of ice an inch or two in thickness, with a chamber of air space beneath it.

Jim took off his wrenched snowshoes, laid them on the crust at the edge of the hole, and pulled himself carefully out till he lay belly-down on the thin ice. Then he warned the dogs back and wriggled his way to shore. As soon as they got below the rapids the river ice was firm again.

He worked to the end of the trap-line by noon and returned to the lower camp with one mink to add to his store of fur. The next day was the 20th—getting near Christmas. Mindful of his promise to be at Waba on the 24th, he took the trail early in the morning, and instead of stopping at Beaver Lake, covered the twenty miles to the head of Long Portage.

As he drew close to his home camp, the following afternoon, he made a bet with himself. "If there's any fur in these last four traps," he promised, "I'll open a can o' peaches an' have a real feast for supper." His imagination grew reckless, then. "If there's two pelts," he told himself, "I'll bake a cake with raisins in it!"

The first trap, like all the others he had visited that day, was empty. "Dog-gone!" he grumbled. "I had my mouth all set for those peaches." He hiked on wearily to the next cubby and gave a whistle of joy. There was a fine mink in the trap. Five minutes later he raised a triumphant yell that set the echoes ringing and the dogs barking. Another mink!

There was one trap left. "Oh well," he chuckled, "let's make it a sporting proposition. If I get anything more, by gosh, I'll frost that cake with sugar icing!"

He approached the blazed tree that marked the location of the last trap-house, and his heart beat fast. With a run of luck like this, there might just possibly be—

"Oh, boy!" he breathed. "Gosh! If it isn't a fisher!"

Never in all his life had he seen such satiny black fur. It was a female, a trifle larger than Miranda, and a far more perfect pelt.

Almost reverently he carried the dark body to the cabin. "Darned if I don't believe that's the finest fisher ever caught in Thunder Bay District!" he murmured in awed tones.

True to his pledge, Jim built a good fire to heat the oven and started mixing his cake. There were no eggs, of course, but he knew how to use plain flour, dried milk and baking powder, and he put in a double handful of raisins. He fed the dogs and prepared the rest of his meal while the cake was baking. It was late when the food was finally ready, and he had not eaten since dawn. But it was worth the wait. His ravenous appetite did full justice to the feast, and no creation of a Waldorf chef ever tasted more delicious than the peaches and raisin cake with which he topped it off.

Jim spent the next day, the 22nd, in camp. He had some clothes to be washed and plenty of fur to skin. When those chores were done he cut and hauled firewood till darkness fell.

In the morning he packed all his cured pelts on the sled and set out southward toward Porcupine Lake. Pat and Bruno seemed to know that a holiday was in the offing. They scampered over the beaten trail, as frisky as the chickadees that sang above them in the spruces. At the lake, Jim swung northeast, following Porcupine River, and spent the night at his shack there.

With the first gray of dawn he roused and sat up in his sleeping-bag. Half awake, he could not at first identify the tingling sense of pleasure that filled him. Then he remembered. Christmas Eve! He hurried through breakfast and harnessed the dogs. "Come on, there, Bruno!" he called jubilantly. "Let's see you travel!"

The trails were well packed and fast. The dogs, plunging eagerly into their collars, made the seven miles back to the lake in an hour, while Jim panted along in their wake. At the head of Porcupine he turned them to the left for the twelve-mile overland trip to Wababimiga. They were no longer moving over level ice, and their pace was necessarily slower, but noonday found them approaching the

Waba cabin. There was a cheerful spire of smoke rising straight upward in the clear, frosty air. Out by the woodpile, one of the girls was singing. Jim cupped his hands and launched a shout that brought an immediate answering hail. When his team pulled into the yard the whole family was out to greet him.

He hugged his mother and sisters and gave Lindsay a resounding slap on the back. "Where'd you come from, kid?" he asked, laughing. "Thought I'd beat you in, for once."

"Not this time," said the younger boy. "I finished a day early an' got here last night. Came down from Poplar Lake with Dad."

Jim looked at his father in surprise. "What!" he exclaimed. "You went up there by yourself?"

Big Lindsay chuckled. "Sure did," said he. "More'n that, I went to town. Trail was good, an' I rode the sled most o' the way."

"Wait till you see what he brought back!" cried Ida. "A turkey—and—"

"Hold on, now, daughter," Mrs. Vanderbeck interrupted. "Don't try to tell everything. Half the fun o' Christmas is being surprised."

That afternoon the boys helped their father finish up such odd jobs as needed doing. Tomorrow there would be no work. When darkness fell, the girls brought out two wreaths of ground pine they had made, and hung them in the front windows. Then a pair of candles were lighted and placed on the broad sills, where they would shine out over the snow.

There was no fireplace in the cabin, and no place to hang up stockings. However, the Vanderbecks had a system for distributing Christmas gifts that was all their own. With a bit of chalk, Lindsay marked out a square on the floor at the foot of each bed place. Then the lights were extinguished except for one dim candle. With a deal of mysterious tiptoeing and giggling, the family went the rounds, depositing such presents as they had. Good-nights were said, the candle put out, and they all went to bed.

A riot of laughter and shouting woke Jim out of dreamless slumber. It was still dark outside but the lamp on the puncheon table had been lighted, and the girls were going from bed to bed crying, "Merry Christmas!"

Big Lindsay sat up with a chuckle. "Brrrr!" he said, his breath rising in a white cloud. "Get that fire goin', somebody! It's colder'n a dog's nose!"

Jim hustled some kindling into the stove and lighted it, while his brother scratched away the frost on the windowpane and looked at the thermometer that hung outside.

"Forty below," he announced. "An' fine, bright starlight. Looks like it would be a nice day."

With the flames roaring in the stove, it didn't take long for the temperature inside the cabin to grow more comfortable, Mrs. Vanderbeck began making gestures toward getting breakfast, but the girls forbade it.

"You know the rule, Ma," they told her laughingly. "Presents come first! Sit down, everybody, and open one at a time."

They took turns, starting with Lindsay, the youngest. No bright ribbons or fancy wrappings adorned these gifts. Even paper was a luxury at Waba, and some of the packages were done up in birchbark and tied with rawhide thongs.

In his pile Jim found a handsome plaid shirt of 22-ounce mackinaw cloth from his father, two pairs of heavy wool socks knitted by the girls, a box of rifle cartridges from Lindsay, and from his mother a pair of double-knit wool mitts with fur trimmed caribou hide gauntlets to cover them. There were also two or three remembrances that had come by mail—among them a book of trout flies from a wealthy sportsman in the States.

The others meanwhile were opening their own presents and holding them up for inspection. Simple, useful articles for the most part, though Big Lindsay had brought the women folks some bits of feminine adornment from Toronto. Jim's gifts to his family were homemade things that he had worked on during his lonely evenings in camp. Deerskin moccasins for his sisters—stout moose hide belts for the two Lindsays—a birchbark sewing basket for his mother.

"A pretty swell Christmas, I call it!" said Ida when the presents had all been exhibited. "And now, Ma, you just sit still while Mary and I get breakfast on the table."

When the low winter sun came up, it was, as Lindsay had prophesied, a fine, clear day. The boys took their rifles down to the lake and held a shooting match—five rounds apiece at 200 yards. Their target was the top of a tin can, six inches in diameter. Each of them drilled it twice after long and careful sighting. They were congratulating each other on their marksmanship when Big Lindsay strolled down to the landing.

"Mind if I try a turn?" he asked. "Don't know's I can do much. Ain't as steady as I used to be, but I might be able to hit a big mark like that."

He raised Jim's rifle and fired five times in quick succession. Four of the shots were clean bull's eyes. The fifth creased the outer edge of the tin. "Yes," he said apologetically, "I've slipped, I guess. Arms were tired on that last one."

"Gosh-all-hemlock!" breathed Jim, in a tone of respect. "I'd like to see you on a day you were good!"

Dinner that day was an event to be remembered. Four hours of busy labor on the part of Mrs. Vanderbeck and the girls went into its preparation. About two o'clock in the afternoon Ida came to the door and announced that everything was ready. The men trooped in from the shed, sniffing hungrily at the warm, fragrant air. A big brown turkey graced the head of the board. Flanking it, on either side, were dishes of mashed potatoes and hubbard squash. In addition there were homemade pickles and preserves and smoking hot biscuits.

Big Lindsay whetted the carving knife. "Ladies an' gentlemen," he said, with an air of ceremony, "be seated."

But just at that moment they heard a faint, approaching jingle of bells. "Must be Santa Claus coming," grinned Jim.

His brother had run to the window. "It's Emile!" he cried. "Set another place at the table, Mary—we've got company!"

They threw the door wide and welcomed the French trapper with halloos and cheers. His fast team of four police dogs came up the trail at a smart trot, and behind them the Vanderbecks could see the flash of Emile's grin in the furred hood of his parka.

"S'prise, eh?" he called. "Merry Christmas, everybody!"

When he had unhitched and chained his dogs, Emile Coté came in and warmed his hands at the fire.

"Take off your things an' set right down," said

Big Lindsay. "I sort o' thought the smell o' that turkey roastin' would be noticeable over in your country."

The boys laughed. Emile's trap-lines lay twenty miles to the east, on the Drowning River.

"I can't smell that far," grinned the Frenchman, "but I got a good calendar." He took his place with the rest at the table. "How you like those bells on my team, eh?" he asked.

"Ought to be grand for scarin' the game," Jim replied. "They do sound nice, though. Sort o' Christmassy."

The high piled plates passed down the line, and for a time they were all too busy for conversation. At last, when even the plum pudding was eaten and the two older men had lighted after dinner pipes, the talk began again.

Emile reported good trapping down the Drowning. "Got four fisher already," he concluded. "Maybe two —three hundred dollars' worth o' fur on my sled."

"I'll bet I caught one animal none o' the rest of you've got," Jim put in. And to the accompaniment of howls of laughter he told them the story of the skunk.

His father moved his chair away in haste. "Hmm!" he remarked. "I thought ye smelled a little high yesterday. Funny, though. That's the first skunk I've heard of in these parts for five years."

The brief winter afternoon passed quickly. They played bridge and other games, chatted and sang songs. After some urging Big Lindsay consented to repeat all nine verses of his poem, "The Ballad of Serpentine Lake; or Johnson and the Moose." He was famous all through New Brunswick and northern Ontario as a maker of rhymes, and the family never tired of hearing them.

When dusk came on and the lamps were lighted, Ida suggested a candy pull. She was soon at work over the stove and the tangy-sweet pungence of cooking molasses filled the room.

"Better get your hands buttered, folks," she announced, at length. "This stuff's 'most ready to pull."

Just then there was a small, timid knock at the door of the cabin. Mary looked at her mother quizzically. "More visitors?" she asked, and went to lift the latch.

A young Indian girl, thin and scared looking, stood on the threshold. She held out a battered tin cup. "You gottem salt?" she asked, in a frightened whisper.

The gathered household stared at her for a moment. Then Mrs. Vanderbeck spoke briskly. "Why, sure," she said. "Come right in!"

They could see a hungry gleam in the girl's eyes as she stepped forward timidly and sniffed the molasses-laden air. Mary smiled at her. "You been celebrating Christmas?" she asked, trying to make conversation.

"No," said the girl.

"Didn't your pa bring you any Christmas presents?"

"No," she said again, shaking her head.

Mrs. Vanderbeck exchanged a glance with her husband. "Well, for the land's sakes!" she murmured compassionately.

Jim saw that the girl, for all her frail smallness, must be fifteen or sixteen years old. She had on a pair of greasy deerskin breeches, a torn cotton dress, and over it a ragged old canvas parka. The hood hung back from her black braids and flat, high-cheek-boned little face.

Ida set the candy pan at the back of the stove and walked across to the curtained closet by her bed.

"I declare," she said, almost violently, "I'm going to give that child my old sweater and a pair of mittens. Look at those hands!"

Mrs. Vanderbeck nodded. "Good idea," she said. "I've got some thick stockings I just finished knitting, too."

So it was that when the dazed Indian girl left the cabin she had not only her borrowed salt but warm wool between her and the biting frost.

They went ahead with their candy pulling when she was gone, but some of the gaiety had gone out of the evening.

"Seems kind of tough on the other five kids—the little ones—doesn't it?" asked Jim. "They're probably as bad off as she is. No Christmas—gosh!"

"I'll tell you what," beamed Mary, flushed and warm from the pulling. "Soon as this is done let's take the candy up to their camp. Dear knows we don't need it, after that dinner!"

The golden strings had already begun to stiffen and lose their stickiness. Mary set the candy in the shed to chill, and the four young Vanderbecks donned their outdoor garments. Emile said he would rather stay and talk to their parents.

"Whee!" cried Lindsay, as he tied on his snow-shoes. "It's cold tonight, all right. But this is going to be fun. Just look at that moon!"

XIV

THE quartet of young people needed no lantern to light their way down the path to the lake. Bright moonlight, reflected from the snow, created a world of ghostly, sparkling white. Behind them in the thick bush, trees cracked in the cold with a sound like gunfire, and they could feel the breath catch, freezing in their nostrils. There was no wind. The steady walking kept them comfortable inside their warm winter clothes. It was a good two miles across the lake to Joe Leake's shack, but after a day indoors they all welcomed the exercise.

"S'pose they'll still be up?" Jim asked. "It's 'most eight o'clock."

"Oh, sure," answered Ida. "The girl wanted that salt for supper I expect, and she's only about an hour ahead of us."

As they drew nearer, they made out the dark bulk of the log cabin in its rough clearing.

"You can't see a light even if they've got one," Ida volunteered. "There's moose hide over the only window. No glass."

She took the lead as they climbed the bank, and rapped with mittened knuckles on the door. There was a rustling noise inside like scurrying mice. Then a voice spoke in a sort of grunt, and a moment later the door creaked open a few inches.

"Hello," said Ida cheerfully. "We've come to wish you all a Merry Christmas, and bring this for the little folks."

Again the grunt from somewhere in the shack and the door was pulled wider. It was the Eskimo woman who stood there holding a dirty blanket about her, her dark figure etched against the light from a smoke crusted oil lamp. She said nothing, but motioned to them to enter.

Inside, with the others, Jim looked about him half fascinated, half disgusted. He had been in Indian houses before, and the thick reek of unwashed bodies was not new to him. The floor looked inches deep in filth—rags, moose hair, bones—all the accumulated trash of a place that was never cleaned. A fire burned dully on a patch of earth at the far end of the hut, and the smoke eddied upward through a small hole in the roof.

Jim nodded to Joe Leake, squatting on one of the bough beds that nearly filled the room. The dark faces of the children peered out from hiding places in the smoky gloom. Ida was putting the opened paper of candy in the squaw's hands.

"It's something to eat," she explained, pointing to her mouth in sign language. "See—you break it, this way." She picked up a bit of the brittle taffy and put it between the lips of the Eskimo.

At the sweet taste, a light broke over her face. She smiled, showing beautiful white teeth, and Jim remembered that Ida had described her as handsomer than most Indians. There was a kind of pride in the way she held herself, and her strange almond-shaped eyes had a look of mystery in their coal-black depths. He could understand the superstitious fear of the Ojibways who thought her a witch.

"For you and the children," Ida finished, smiling and pointing. "Come on, kids. Let's go along so they can enjoy it."

*   *   *   *

Led by the silvery chime of Emile's bells, their dog sleds set out from Wababimiga for town, the morning after Christmas. It was another clear, bright day, and the well-broken trail over the lake ice made perfect going. Big Lindsay rode the French trapper's sled, sitting on the piled-up furs and warmly wrapped against the cold. Behind came Jim's team, augmented by one of Lindsay's huskies, and three dogs from the

Vanderbecks' home camp pulled the third toboggan. There were six people in the party. Mrs. Vanderbeck had no relish for the seventy-mile round trip on snow-shoes. She had sent them all off with her blessing, and said she would be glad to stay at the cabin and keep the home fires burning.

After their long evening of fun they had slept late that morning. It was midday when they reached the long carry, and nearing dark when they came out on Poplar Lake. They crossed to Lindsay's camp, and there, by dint of some crowding, made themselves comfortable for the night. It was a holiday trip. Hard beds and cramped quarters were part of the fun, and they took it all hilariously.

An early start got them into Nakina at two o'clock the next afternoon. When the pelts had been unloaded at the storehouse, they took their duffel on up the track to their summer home. Then the boys and their father came back to greet various friends around the station. That night Mr. Vanderbeck made up an order for provisions and sent it off to the supply house in Port Arthur. A buyer from one of the great fur companies was expected in three days, and by the time the food arrived there would be money to pay for it.

There was good skiing on the long gravel hill to the west of town. Glad of the company of boys their own age, Jim and Lindsay spent most of the next two days sailing down the steep slope on their homemade

skis. The evening of the 30th the fur buyer got off the
Limited, and word of his coming spread quickly from
house to house. He established headquarters in the
main room of the little frame hotel.

By daylight next morning the trappers were as-
sembling with their packs of furs. The buyer was a
shrewd, gray-haired little Frenchman who had been
in the business a long time. He spoke half a dozen
Indian dialects as well as English and French, and he
could spot a blemish in a carefully camouflaged pelt
as far as he could see it.

Big Lindsay sat listening to the first few sales, gos-
siping meanwhile with Emile, the Lagarde boys and
other acquaintances.

"Prices are good," he announced at length. "I notice
he's been payin' eleven dollars for average mink, an'
that young Finn just got eighty for his silver fox.
Ermine are only fifty cents, though."

It was soon the Vanderbecks' turn. There was no
haggling. Once or twice the boys' father called attention to a particularly fine skin and the price was
raised a dollar or two. In all, their early season's catch
brought $510. This included 11 mink, $120; 48
ermine, $24; 3 fisher, $165; 2 marten, $52; 6 fox,
$72; 2 lynx, $40; 1 timber wolf, $25, and 1 coyote,
$12. In addition, the boys had already gone to the
warden and proved their claim to wolf bounties of
$25 each.

TRAP-LINES NORTH

"Well boys," said Mr. Vanderbeck, as he stuffed the roll of bills into his purse, "do as well the rest o' the winter an' I reckon we'll come through."

The family stayed in town over the holiday, and had their New Year's dinner at the home of a married sister. The following day the freight from Port Arthur brought the supplies they had ordered. They spent the afternoon getting them home and repacking them on the toboggans. And before daylight on the morning of the 3d, they were ready to start hauling back to the bush.

It was bitter cold as the two boys mushed down the track in the teeth of the wind. They beat their arms to start the warm blood circulating, and pulled the furred hoods close around their faces. The thermometer on the wall of the station stood at forty-three below.

They plodded down the long white sweep of Cordingley Lake, where the stinging wind caught their breath and turned it to hoarfrost. When they got to the shelter of the woods along Cranberry River the traveling was easier.

"If it gets much colder," Jim panted through stiffened lips, "the dogs won't go."

Lindsay nodded and plowed ahead. Half a mile farther on he stopped, pointing a mittened hand toward the north bank. Jim saw a gray-black animal running at the edge of the woods. A silver fox. He fumbled with the deerskin cover of his rifle but before he could bring it into action, the fox had dived out of sight in the bush.

"Too bad that one got away," he told his brother. "I saw the fur buyer giving seventy or eighty bucks for silver fox. Why didn't you try a shot?"

Lindsay patted the rifle under his arm and shook his head. "Bolt action," he said. "Froze up. Have to thaw it out."

Two deer crossed the ice ahead of them, as they came out on Poplar Lake. Jim wondered again, as he had often done, how such thin-legged, short-haired creatures could live through a winter in those bitter latitudes.

The boys got to Lindsay's camp before dusk. With a big fire roaring in the stove, the cabin was soon warm. Meanwhile they had unloaded the provisions and put the dogs in their kennels. The wind went down as darkness came, but the dry, still cold was unabated.

In the morning they hitched up the teams and started back to Nakina. The dogs whined in the cruel chill of dawn. Several times, on the trip to town, they lay down in their harness and refused to move. On Jim's sled there was a whip which he rarely used— a homemade affair with a short wooden stock and a fifteen-foot rawhide lash. Grimly he uncoiled it now, and stood over the dogs. They couldn't stay there and freeze to death.

"Hup, you!" he shouted, and laid into their furry backs with a stinging crack of the rawhide.

Bruno got to his feet reluctantly and the others followed. When they reached the head of Cordingley Lake and hit the overland trail to the settlement there was no more lagging. The dogs knew they were nearing home and wanted to run. Jim and Lindsay came whooping into the dooryard, riding the sleds, with both teams going at full gallop.

The temperature continued to fall that night. For the next two days it hung in the neighborhood of 50 below, and there was no use trying to haul supplies. Jim hiked down the track for the mail but was glad to get back inside the snug log house.

It was the 6th of January before the weather moderated enough to travel. That day Jim and his father took another load to Poplar Lake, and on the 7th Big Lindsay went on to Waba while the boy returned to town. There was a day's delay there, for a parcel of clothing to come from the mail-order house, but on the morning of the 9th Jim and Lindsay set out for their trapping grounds with the final load of supplies. The girls kept two of the dogs and stayed on in Nakina, waiting for one last package to arrive.

Jim was glad, as always, to get back into the bush.

"Funny, isn't it?" he said to Lindsay that night, in the cabin on Poplar Lake. "I was crazy to get to town after Christmas. Seemed like the sweetest sound 1 could hear would be the old Limited whistlin', up the track. Right now I'd rather hear a wolf howl or a fox bark than all the engines on the C. N. R.!"

They struck east to Wababimiga next morning and made such good time that they came out of the woods at the head of the lake by noon.

Half a mile away on the north shore, smoke was rising from a cabin half hidden by spruces. "Dad's line camp," said Lindsay. "Somebody's there. Let's go over."

A tall, familiar figure came out on the ice as they approached and threw up an arm in greeting. "Thought you boys might be along today," said their father, "I was gettin' ready to pull a net. Bait's runnin' low, what with all these pet critters your Ma's been feedin'."

"You leave it to us," Jim replied. "That's too heavy a job for an invalid to tackle alone. Come on Lindsay, bring your ax and we'll get Dad some fish."

Two poles, sticking up out of the ice ninety feet apart, marked the ends of the net. They had been set in late October, before the lake froze. With their axes, the boys cut away the ice around each pole. It was a long task, for one of the holes had to be made wide enough to pull the net through, and they went down a good three feet before striking water. When both openings were chopped out, Jim pulled one pole

up from the mud, untied the net and made it fast
to a long rope, the other end of which was tied to the
pole, laid flat on the ice.

Then both boys went to the opposite stake and
pulled it up. Hand over hand they hauled the net out
on the ice, while the slack of the rope followed it beneath the surface. Caught in the mesh were nearly
thirty fish. Suckers, whitefish, bullheads and four
huge pike made a glistening heap in the snow.

When the net had been straightened out Jim went
back to the other hole and hauled the rope back.
The end of the net was then tied to its stake once
more, and both poles were thrust firmly into the lake
bottom. In half an hour the ice would freeze around
them and they would be fast again.

They stopped at the cabin to warm themselves and
brew a pot of tea. Then, with the fish on Big Lindsay's
sled, they mushed their dog teams down the lake to
the family's main camp.

Marten

XV

FOR the three days that the boys spent at Waba, the fine winter weather continued. It was cold, of course. Twenty to thirty degrees below zero was the normal temperature for that time of year. But neither dogs nor humans minded such weather. They put in the time profitably, cutting and hauling firewood, visiting their father's traps to the south of the lake and mending snowshoes and dog harness.

Meanwhile the girls had returned from Nakina, and in the evenings the cabin rang with their good times. The night of the 14th, Big Lindsay lighted his pipe and stretched his long legs beside the stove.

"You boys plannin' to start back tomorrow?" he asked.

"I was," Jim answered. "Why? Anything you want me to do?"

"No, I was just thinkin' the three of us might cruise up north o' your country an' see how the fur sign looks. Used to be an old trap-line in there. Don't believe it's been worked for four—five years."

"Fine!" said Jim. "Think you ought to undertake a trip like that, yet?"

"Huh!" his father grinned. "Reckon I can keep up with any young shavers 'round here! You an' Lindsay get your duffel ready. We'll get off early."

So it came about that the three of them left Waba before daybreak next morning. Jim cut straight across to his line at Porcupine Lake with his own dogs, while the two Lindsays took another team and followed a more roundabout route to the east.

Crossing the high ground between the lakes, Jim sighted a good-sized bull moose feeding in the poplar thickets. Otherwise the trip was made without incident, and he reached Porcupine in time to make the circuit of the lake, tending his traps.

In the last one he visited there was a mink. Carrying it proudly he crossed the ice, heading for his cabin, and saw Lindsay and his father coming through the dusk.

"Hi, there!" he shouted. "Look what I got!"

[163]

Lindsay laughed. "Look what we got!" he answered, and held up another mink that might have been the twin brother of Jim's.

"Pretty good day's work," the elder Vanderbeck remarked. "But you'll have to catch plenty in the next couple o' weeks. Breedin' season'll be comin' soon, an' the best o' the fur won't take bait from then on."

It snowed that night and the flakes were still drifting down steadily when Jim crawled out of bed to light the morning fire.

"Want to lay up here till it's over?" he asked his father.

But the big woodsman sniffed at the air and shook his head. "This won't last more'n another hour or two," he said. "How deep is it out there?"

"Plenty deep," Jim replied. "Must be a foot of new snow—real light and soft."

"Well, we can make it to your main camp, anyhow," his father decided.

The boys took turns at breaking trail ahead of the sleds, and they reached Squaw River by midday. Sure enough, the snow had stopped falling and the low sun shone through breaking clouds.

Jim and Lindsay built a fire in the stove and left their father in the cabin while they went down river along the trap line. Many of the cubbies were buried so deep that the boys had to dig out around them, using their snowshoes as shovels. It was hard work. When they had finished excavating a trap-house three or four miles below camp, Lindsay mopped his damp forehead with his sleeve. "Look at that," he grumbled. "Not even a nibble at the bait. I don't believe there's any fur down this way anyhow."

"Guess not," Jim answered with a grin. "Must be all the animals have hiked off up river to your country. Well, it's getting late. You start along back. I'm only going to look at one more."

Fifty paces up a nearby brook he had made a water-set weeks before. The blaze on a spruce above the bank showed him where it was, and he knelt down, pulling the snow away with his mittened hands. The trap was no longer on the log. He found the stake and followed up the chain link by link. Then a sweep of his gauntlet uncovered soft brown fur. He pulled up the trap and chuckled as he took out a fine big mink.

The light in the cabin window made a welcome yellow beacon, as he plodded up the trail through the dark. Trapping was a lot more fun, he decided, when you had your own folks for company.

They struck north next morning under bright, cold stars. After half a dozen miles of heavy breaking through the heart of the bush, they came to a good-sized brook.

"This looks like it," said Big Lindsay. "Cast around

a little an' see if there's any blazes."

The boys had not hunted long before Jim's keen eyes picked out a weathered gray spot the size of his hand on the side of a tree. He gave the "Coo-ee" call that he and Lindsay always used in the woods, and soon the two dog teams came straining along in his snowshoe tracks.

Constantly, as they plowed along northward, the eyes of the three woodsmen searched the snow. Occasionally a rabbit track crossed their trail but that was all. At sunset Big Lindsay called a halt.

"It's been more'n twenty-four hours since the snow stopped," he said. "If there was any fur 'round here we'd see sign before this. Well, it's too far to go back. Better get started on a camp for the night."

Sleeping out comfortably in January on the Hudson Bay slope requires a certain skill. But the boys knew what to do. The first thing was to find a big tree with some open space around it. A short distance up the brook they came on a huge old pine, nearly three feet through at the butt. Jim took an ax and went after poles, while Lindsay and his father scooped away the snow from in front of the tree. They cleared an area as large as a small room, piling the snow in a yard-deep bank around it. Then they scattered the ground thickly with balsam boughs. By this time Jim was back with a dozen long, straight poles, which he proceeded to brace against the tree in a semicircle.

[166]

The sled-canvas from the two toboggans was now brought and wrapped around the poles to make a sort of lean-to.

"That looks snug enough," Big Lindsay gave his approval. "All we need now is the fire."

In ten minutes the boys had a bright blaze going in a hollow between two roots and close against the big tree. And almost at once, the reflected heat began to warm the shelter. They cooked supper, fed the dogs and bedded them down with dry boughs, and were ready to spread their sleeping-bags on the soft, springy balsam. A low barrier of snow protected their beds from the fire.

"There," grunted the elder Vanderbeck contentedly. "Put on a couple o' big chunks, so she'll burn all night, an' we'll sleep as warm as summer."

It was a trifle chilly crawling out in the morning, with the fire dead and the temperature 30 below. However, Jim had prepared a pile of dry pine kindling the night before. It was only a moment's work to get the blaze going again.

For two days they continued to cruise the region, taking different directions in order to cover more ground. They were far beyond the abandoned trapline now. Jim might have been thrilled by the knowledge that he was exploring country where possibly white men had never been before. But that was no new experience for him, and the scarcity of fur sign disappointed him. Also the constant effort of breaking trail was hard and tiring. It was with a sense of relief that they headed back toward the Squaw, with the unset traps still on their sleds.

After a night in Jim's home camp the three bade each other good-bye. Lindsay went westward toward his own ground. Their father started the homeward trip to Waba. And Jim, piling supplies on his toboggan, took the trail down river. It was high time he was getting over his line again.

* * * *

Now, in the dead of the far northern winter, one day was much like another. There was a rhythm to living which gave the boy plenty to occupy his strong young body, and left his mind free to think and plan.

If the weather was clear he got out of his bough bed about 5:30 in the morning, hustled into his outer clothes and started a fire in the tin camp stove. While the flames were taking hold of the dry wood, he filled two pails with snow and set them on the stove to melt. Then he carefully rolled up his eiderdown sleeping-bag, wrapped it in its tarpaulin and set about getting breakfast.

Usually he made himself a bowl of oatmeal porridge, which he ate with milk powder, dissolved in water, and a little sugar. He carried prunes, dried apples or dried peaches in his grub box, and a handful

[168]

of these gave some balance to his diet. He ate bread if he had it, or made a corn meal johnny cake and fried a strip of bacon. Butter was something he had learned to do without. A pan of cocoa or tea completed the meal.

When the tin dishes were washed and repacked in the grub box, it was time to take the trail. The toboggan, leaned up against the shack for the night, was laid in the snow, with the dog harness stretched in front of it. The sled-canvas was spread out flat and the packing began.

Next to the upcurled nose of the toboggan Jim placed the dog pail, with a sack of corn meal and four or five spare traps inside it. Back of the pail came the folded 7-by-10 wall tent which he usually carried for emergencies. Then the heavy grub box, containing food and utensils. A bundle of frozen fish, for baiting traps and feeding the dogs, was placed next, and behind it the pack-sack, filled with clothes and small necessities. Riding the tail of the sled was the folding tin stove, with its telescope pipe.

Jim laid the bed-roll lengthwise on top, and pulled the sides of the canvas up around the load. Starting from the front, he lashed it tight and thrust his rifle under the lacings. The ax was put in front, under the nose of the toboggan.

One at a time he led the dogs from their huts behind the cabin and harnessed them, Bruno first, then

[169]

Paddy. The chains were thrown into the dog pail, and Jim moved out ahead of the team on his snowshoes. Breaking trail in heavy snow, he was lucky to make two miles an hour; and visiting the traps took additional time. As he came to each one, he looked to see if it was sprung, brushed the loose snow away, and made sure the bait had not been stolen.

Sometimes he would find half a dozen traps in a row untouched. Then he might come to three or four together that held the bodies of gorbies, squirrels and rabbits. Still there was always the chance of discovering a mink or a marten frozen between the steel jaws.

Unless he was in a hurry, Jim stopped at noon for a bite of lunch. He stripped the boughs from two or three small trees for the dogs to lie on, took such supplies as he needed out of the grub box, and turned the toboggan up on its side to keep the snow from freezing to the bottom. When his fire was going, he made a pot of tea and thawed out his bread, if he had any. With a slice of bacon in the pan, he fried a piece of dry moose meat. It was hard to chew, but it tasted good to a hungry man in the woods.

His meal over, he repacked the load on the sled and continued down the river. About four in the afternoon, if he had timed his day's journey accurately, he drew near one of his line camps. While there was still light enough to see, he dug out the dog huts with a snowshoe, brought the chains from the sled, unharnessed the dogs, and fastened each one in his kennel. The harness was hung up on a peg inside the cabin. Then the sled was unpacked, the duffel carried in, and the toboggan itself set up on end against the house.

The next chore was to feed the dogs. While the fire in the stove was warming the cabin, Jim built another one outside and hung the dog pail, half full of snow, over the flames. As soon as the water was hot, he threw in some corn meal and a couple of fish, stirring the mush till the meal was cooked. Then, setting the pail in the snow to cool, he got ready for his own supper. His hands had to be washed in snow, with a cake of soap he carried in his possible-sack. When they were clean he dug frozen mashed potatoes out of a can, warmed up some baked beans, and chopped moose meat with the ax to make hamburger. Bread or bannock with brown sugar was his dessert.

Jim's utensils were few, but they served all his needs. Besides the tin plate and cup, the hunting knife and iron fork and spoon, he had a frying pan, a straight-sided copper teapot, and a five-pound lard pail, used as a kettle. While his supper cooked, he found time to take the corn meal and fish out to the dogs. The food was portioned out, half to each, with a wooden paddle, and the hungry animals rushed at it savagely. Jim could sympathize with them. He felt more or less wolfish himself at the end of a long day.

It was only by a conscious effort that he kept from gobbling his food, when he was all alone in the cabin.

When the meal was finished, and he had washed the dishes in a frying pan full of snow water, he skinned such fur as he had caught that day. Then he made himself comfortable on the bough bed and read a while or wrote up his diary by candlelight. He had whittled a paddle out of a spruce chip, and sharpened the small end, so that it could be thrust into chinks between the logs. His candle was stuck firmly on the paddle with a drop of hot wax. When he needed the light in any part of the room he simply shoved the wedge of wood into a convenient cranny.

Bedtime was when he felt sleepy—ordinarily about 8:30. He stripped to his heavy woolen underwear, slid into the eiderdown, and pulled the tarpaulin up around it. A minute or two later he was soundly and dreamlessly asleep.

* * * *

By the 23d of January, Jim had covered his trap-line as far down as the burnt land beyond the lower camp, visited the cubbies around Beaver Lake, and made his way back to the lean-to at the head of the long carry. All day there had been a warm heaviness in the air. For the first time in months the snow felt wet and soft. It clung soggily to his snowshoes and doubled the labor of breaking trail.

[172]

He woke in the night to an unfamiliar sound—the drum of rain on a part of the roof where the snow had melted. That meant there would be no traveling tomorrow. He turned over contentedly and went to sleep again.

The first day of inactivity passed pleasantly enough. Jim loafed around camp, mended his dog harness, washed a few clothes. Outside the temperature stayed well above the freezing mark, and water dripped steadily from the sodden trees. Luckily, the boy had brought along a couple of books in his possible-sack. When he had performed all the chores he could think of, he sprawled near the open front of the cabin and read.

The following morning it had stopped raining, but the air was, if anything, even warmer. He put on his snowshoes and made a try at walking along the trail, but the snow was so heavy with water that it was almost impossible to move. Out on the river he could see a foot-deep morass of soft slush.

There was still another restless day in camp before the wind swung into the north and the weather began to turn colder. When Jim woke on the morning of the 27th, there were icicles hanging in a fringe from the lean-to roof, and the air had a real nip to it. Eagerly the boy dressed, got breakfast and prepared to take the trail. As soon as the dogs were harnessed, he led the way down the bank to the river. "Come on now,

[173]

Bruno, old boy!" he called cheerfully. "Let's see you mush!"

The big lead dog was as keen for action as his master, but he had a hard time keeping up. Where the thin crust on top of the slush would bear Jim's long snowshoes, it broke under the dogs' weight. Their floundering progress was soon made more difficult by balls of slush freezing to their feet and weighting down the fur along their bellies. When Jim came back to scrape the ice off their toes, he realized it was useless to go on. Nothing for it but to wait another day.

For twenty-four hours the temperature continued to drop. It was so cold that night that Jim built a shelter of boughs across the front of the lean-to and kept up a roaring fire in the stove. At daybreak he found the crust solid enough to hold his weight, even without snowshoes. His imprisonment was over at last.

XVI

THE toboggan ran smoothly and easily over the icy surface. Occasionally the dogs slipped, but they had little real pulling to do. They were still fresh and eager when they trotted up to Jim's home camp that afternoon.

The boy cut firewood until dark, and then refilled his grub box from the supply of provisions in the cabin. He was impatient to get down to his Porcupine River line while the clear weather held.

Up at dawn next morning, he led his team across to the south-bound trail and hit a fast pace through the frosty woods. The cold had sharpened. When the sun came through the trees it glittered on a million ice-sheathed twigs. Even the hardy whisky-jacks were silent for once, and Jim knew that when they sought shelter it was a cold day.

He found a red fox in one of the traps on the south shore of Porcupine Lake. It was the first fur he had caught since before the thaw, and though the skin would be worth only five or six dollars, he regarded it as a good omen. Ordinarily a fox was smarter and harder to trap than most other animals.

Jim carried the frozen body to the toboggan and was kneeling to reset the trap when the dogs began barking behind him. Another sound reached him faintly through the flaps of his aviator's helmet. A voice calling? He whirled to stare out across the lake and saw a dog team coming at a gallop, the driver riding the toboggan and waving his arm.

It was young Lindsay. He would have known that black-and-white leader of his brother's anywhere. With a loud whoop, he flung down the trap and ran out to meet the approaching sled.

"For gosh sakes!" he shouted in delight. "How'd you get down here? Thought you were way up around Poplar Lake somewhere!"

"Hi, big boy!" grinned the youngster. "I aimed to give you a surprise, only I wasn't sure just where I'd find you. Got an early start from my lower camp this morning, an' when you weren't at your place I picked up the fresh trail heading this way. Where you bound? Going to Waba?"

[176]

"Maybe I will tomorrow, if I can get over the lower line," Jim replied. "Come on an' go with me."

They traveled down Porcupine River in company that afternoon. When they reached Jim's lean-to camp a mink and several ermine had been added to the fur on the toboggan.

Jim looked at the half-open cabin and shivered. "Golly, Peter!" he muttered, thrashing his arms. "It's colder'n blue blazes tonight. Think we'll keep alive in there? You'd better cut some poles an' close in the front while I unhitch the dogs."

Back of the lean-to, in the shelter of a clump of thick young spruce, he dug out deep hollows in the snow and filled them with boughs. It was the best he could do for the dogs. He knew they would burrow into the spruce tips, curl up into furry balls, and keep warm somehow.

Lindsay had closed off the front of the cabin with poles and brush, and once they had a fire going in the tin stove, the frigid temperature inside began to rise. Even so it was so cold when they went to bed that a pail of snow water six feet from the stove had a skim of ice on it. Half a dozen times in the night Jim woke, shivering, to put another chunk of wood on the fire.

At daybreak the boys hustled into their clothes. "If the dogs'll move, in this cold," Jim spoke, through chattering teeth, "we'd better hit out for Waba. We'd freeze solid in the tent if we tried to camp down below."

They gulped some hot tea and dragged the teams out of their bough nests. Reluctantly the dogs consented to make a start. When they had covered two or three miles a light wind sprang up from the south and the cold began to moderate. A haze came over the sky. There was a storm on the way.

It was more than twenty miles to the family's camp on Wababimiga, but on the hard crust the going was fast. The boys got in before dark, just as the first flakes of snow began to fill the air.

Big Lindsay was lying down when they came bursting into the warm, lamp-lit room. He looked thin and haggard, with a shaggy growth of beard on his face.

Jim stopped in surprise. "What's the matter, Dad?" he asked.

The big woodsman gave him a twisted grin. "Must have got too ambitious, takin' that trip with you fellows," he replied. "Been crippled up, here, ever since I got back."

"It's a good thing you boys came," Mrs. Vanderbeck remarked. Her usually placid countenance wore a sober look. "The girls have managed to keep us in wood," she went on, "but the traps haven't been tended for two weeks. I don't know what possessed

[178]

that man to go gallivantin' off in the bush when he's
hardly home from the hospital—"

"Don't worry now, Ma," Ida put in. "We'll make
out fine, with Jim and Lindsay here. You know Dad's
felt better today, and all he needs is a good rest."

It snowed heavily all that night and most of the
next day. The boys performed such outdoor chores
as there were to be done, and stayed quietly in the
cabin the rest of the time. Bread was being baked,
and it filled the snug log house with a tantalizing
fragrance. Jim read aloud to his father a while, and
in the afternoon the four young people played a few
rubbers of bridge.

About dusk it stopped snowing and the wind
switched into the west. Jim took a homemade snow
shovel and went out to clear off the platform in front
of the cabin. More than a foot of snow had fallen in
twenty-four hours, and he found it drifted above the
window-sills and half way up the batten door. It
would be heavy breaking tomorrow. As he finished
shoveling off the platform he glanced out to the west,
up the lake, and stopped suddenly, staring. In the
pale evening light the islands stood out, sharply black.
Between the point and the nearest island, a bobbing
gray speck was moving across the white waste. The
distance must have been more than half a mile, but
Jim was certain his eyes had not deceived him. Only
one animal would make that kind of leaping, floun-

dering advance through deep snow. A timber wolf.

Jim ran to the door. "Hey, Lindsay," he called, "get me my rifle—quick!" But by the time the weapon had been passed out to him, the wolf was nearly out of sight behind the southern point. He made a hasty adjustment of the sights and brought the rifle to his shoulder. Too late. Another of those long bounds had carried the animal into concealment beyond the woods.

"Mighty big wolf," the boy muttered to himself. "Wonder where he was coming from. Must have passed awful close by Joe Leake's camp."

✤   ✤   ✤   ✤

The first day of February dawned bright and fair. With so much to be done, the boys decided to split up the work. Lindsay was to cut wood and look after the traps close to camp. Jim undertook to visit the more distant lines. He packed a couple of days' rations in the knapsack, took his ax and rifle and set out along the trail to the east. The snow was so deep it would have slowed him up to take the dogs. Even on his big seven-foot winter snowshoes it was no fun breaking trail.

He dug out one cubby after another without finding any fur. It was not till he had left the Wababimiga River and was plowing along the overland trail to his father's south camp that he took anything worthwhile out of the traps. Then luck came in an avalanche. He found a marten and two mink caught, all within a few hundred yards of each other.

Camping that night in Big Lindsay's lean-to, Jim decided next morning to take a different route home. He knew the Waba camp lay almost due west, a dozen miles away, and though he had never traveled that exact course before, he felt pretty sure he could come out close to his destination.

He finished his breakfast, slipped his shoulders into the pack-straps and put on the long, sharp-toed snowshoes. For the first mile or two he followed the narrow, winding brook that ran past his father's line camp. Then, as the brook channel strayed away to the left, he took a straight line overland through the bush. It was a pretty country—level and fairly open. The sun came slanting across the snow, edging the dark spruces with golden light.

About noon Jim emerged from the woods at the edge of a strip of burnt land. The fire must have gone over the area years before, for a sturdy growth of poplar saplings now covered the ground. Between their shimmering gray stems he could see a dark mass, some distance away to the north. Watching it quietly for several seconds he thought he caught a movement. Then the mass separated into two distinct shapes. A pair of moose, feeding in the poplar scrub. He made a mental note to hunt this part of the country next

September, and moved on across the burn. There were dozens of moose trails, all made since the last snow—deep prints where the animals had waded through the drifts on their long stilts of legs.

The burned-over section was not wide, and half an hour's steady hiking brought the boy to green spruce woods again. If his calculations were right he must be within four or five miles of the lake, now. It could not be far to the end of a short trap-line that ran east from behind the camp.

He went ahead more slowly, his eyes alert to pick up familiar landmarks. The land dipped in a gradual slope to the edge of a muskeg, and Jim skirted it, bearing to the north. Right ahead of him, at the foot of a big spruce, he saw a place where the snow had been trampled deep and splashed with red. A few steps brought him alongside the spot. Half buried in the tumbled snow was the body of a young buck deer, torn and bloody. And all about it were the tracks of a monster wolf.

Jim needed only one glance to tell him that this was the work of his old acquaintance—the lone gray killer of the Squaw. The wolf he had seen crossing the lake at dusk, two days before, had been heading this way. He had no doubt now that he had missed a shot at the big fellow himself. Curious, he followed the back trail of the wolf and the deer. The chase must have covered some distance, for the buck's leaps

[182]

had been short and weary toward the end. But the wolf—Jim's eyes bulged as he looked at those tracks. Three full snowshoe lengths between the deep hollows where he had taken off and landed! Twenty feet and more at a bound, in snow that must have been half way to his shoulders!

When he had killed and fed, the gray hunter had gone off at a more leisurely pace into the muskeg. Jim hesitated, half tempted to follow that trail. If there had been plenty of food in his pack he might have done it. But his supplies were gone, and he knew it would take days for the craftiest hunter to get within gunshot of such a wolf as this. Regretfully he took his bearings by the setting sun and pushed on westward. A few minutes later a blazed tree showed him he had reached the trap-line. And before dark he was coming down past the dog kennels into the cabin clearing.

While the boys skinned their fur that night, Jim told about what he had found.

"You think it was the same one?" Lindsay asked.

"Sure of it," the older boy replied. "I measured the tracks. There aren't two wolves like that in this country."

Big Lindsay joined the conversation. "Shouldn't wonder if it was the same wolf I saw on the Little Current River, four years ago. Big as a moose. Tommy Blackfox was with me and you know how

Indians are, about anything queer in the woods. He started mutterin' about witch-wolves. Said bullets wouldn't hurt 'em, and a lot of such stuff!"

"You heard Emile tell how the track Indians were all worked up about this Eskimo woman of Joe Leake's?" asked young Lindsay. "They say she turns into a witch-wolf, nights, and goes around lookin' for papoose meat."

His father snorted. "Sounds like their fool talk," he said. "There's liable to be trouble if they hear this big fellow's hangin' around."

Jim had an uneasy feeling as he listened. His memory flashed back to the wolf he had seen on the lake—coming across on a bee-line from the Cree's cabin. But he kept his own counsel. It was ridiculous even to let such a thought enter his mind. If the animal did seem to hang around the Indian camp, the scent of all that fresh-killed moose meat would be reason enough.

"Let's play a few hands of bridge," he said, and took the stretcher with the marten skin out to the shed to freeze.

❈   ❈   ❈   ❈

During the next two days the boys tended their father's trap-line along the shore of Wababimiga. Ida took a dog team and packed supplies up the ice to the line camp at the head of the lake. She had a good

[184]

supper waiting for them each evening when they came in off the trail. Between them they caught two mink and three or four ermine. The third day they followed another line to the north, between high, rugged hills, crowned with hardwood trees. Tracks of deer and moose were abundant all through this country but they found nothing of value in the traps.

"I doubt if we'll get much more good fur," Jim remarked as they started back in the afternoon. "It's well into February and the breeding season's started. That about ends the mink and fisher for this winter."

But within a mile of the cabin Jim found something that changed his mind. It was a fresh, clean fisher track in the snow. Both boys had the same thought at once.

"Let's hunt him!" said Lindsay. "This time o' year they travel for miles and won't den up."

"Good idea," Jim nodded. "Think we've got enough grub? It may take a day or two, you know."

That night they filled their pack-sacks with such food as Ida could spare them. "Tell Dad we'll be home about day after tomorrow," Lindsay told his sister. "We're goin' to get us one more fisher to wind the season up right."

"Don't be too sure," Ida advised him. "I've heard Emile tell about fisher hunts. Sometimes they get away."

Long before dawn they shouldered their heavy

packs and set forth in the frosty dark. The fisher tracks led straightaway to the north toward the hills. They were easy to follow. The animal had taken its time, stopping now and again to investigate a rabbit path. Once they saw where it had turned off a few yards, lured by the scent of bait in a trap-house. But after circling the cubby a few times, the fisher had resumed its northward journey.

About midday they came to a place where their quarry had killed a snowshoe rabbit. The signs of the struggle were plain in the snow, and a red-stained path showed how the fisher had dragged its victim to a hollow log and denned up for a time.

The tracks leading on from the log were several hours fresher than those they had been following.

"I bet he's not far off now!" cried Lindsay. "Come on—we're gaining on him!"

They made no stop for lunch but held to the trail steadily all afternoon. When the dark began to creep through the trees, the track still stretched temptingly away before them.

"Wish we had a flashlight," Lindsay grumbled. "We're right back of him now."

Jim laughed. "Haven't you had enough for one day?" he asked. "We've been breaking trail for twenty-five miles, and if you want to catch your fisher tomorrow you'd better get some rest."

They pitched an outdoor camp with a bough shel-

ter and a canvas Jim had brought in his pack. The
fire was built at the base of a big tree, and, cold as
it was, they were tired enough to sleep.

Lindsay woke first, at five o'clock next morning.
"Come on!" he urged, pummeling Jim's sleeping-bag.
"It'll be light enough to see, by the time we get some
breakfast."

In an hour they were on the trail again, their backs
to the graying sky in the southeast.

"Know where we are?" Jim asked, as he plodded
in his brother's wake.

"I know we ought to hit Squaw River any minute,
from the distance we've come," Lindsay replied.

"Don't think so," said Jim. "He's been bearing to
the east, the last few miles. I recognized a couple of
places we passed last night, and unless I miss my guess
we're over west of Whitefish Lake—not more'n three-
four miles from my home camp!"

"Well, go up there if you want to," the younger
boy growled. "I'm following this son-of-a-gun till I
get a shot at him."

Jim chuckled. "Keep your shirt on, kid," he said.
"It may be a long time yet. You know Michel Lagarde
hunted one clear to the Albany once—two hundred
miles right across country. This one here looks to me
like he's heading for Hudson Bay."

Before sunrise they crossed Jim's trail from the
Squaw to Whitefish Lake and pushed on into the

wilderness that lay to the south of Ground Hog Rapids. The fisher track seemed no fresher than it had been the day before, and owing to the nature of the country it was harder to follow. Repeatedly they found themselves checked by thick clumps of young spruce—rabbit bush, as they called it. No use trying to cut their way through. They had to cast patiently around the thicket, like a pair of hounds that had lost the scent. Eventually one of them would pick up the outgoing trail, call to the other, and they would plow ahead as far as the next obstacle.

By midafternoon they found the fisher's course had swung definitely to the eastward. Once or twice the trail doubled back a short distance, only to go on again.

"He knows we're after him," Jim said. "It won't be long now. He's scared and worn out."

But nightfall found them still behind their quarry. They made another camp, this time on the lower Porcupine River, somewhere miles to the east of Jim's lean-to.

"If we don't catch up with him tomorrow, the grub'll be gone," Lindsay reported dolefully. "I only hope he's as tuckered out as I am. If he is, he's resting right now!"

Ermine

XVII

THE third day of the hunt brought a change in the fisher's tactics. The boys found where the tired animal had curled up to sleep in the lee of a thicket. From that point on the fresh trail ran in wide, irregular circles.

"He's forgot all about where he was going," said Jim, striding grimly along the track. "All he can think of now is to get away."

That morning the older boy hit a pace that made Lindsay almost trot to keep up. "I'm not going to waste three days an' then give up without even a sight of him," he explained, when his brother voiced a panting remonstrance. "What I'm afraid of now is that he'll find a hole somewhere and we'll lose him. Got to keep him on the run."

The fisher had made another desperate swing that crossed the Porcupine not far from Jim's lower camp. Half a mile beyond, the trail led into a dense tangle of fallen trees and brush, and the boys took separate routes, as usual, to find the track where it emerged. When they met on the other side, Jim held up a warning hand. "Sure you didn't pass any track?" he whispered.

Lindsay shook his head.

"Then he's denned up here!" the older boy announced jubilantly. He pulled Lindsay to a little distance and watched the thicket while he talked. "If he's got a hole in there," he said, "he's got us licked. The law won't let you dig out a fisher or smoke him out. Only thing we can do then is set a couple o' traps an' go home."

"He's way out of his country," the younger brother answered. "Doesn't seem likely he'd know of any hole here unless he found it by dumb luck."

"Just what I think," Jim nodded. "So here's what we can try. Take a look at that brush heap. It's pretty open all around it except one place where I came through, over to the west there. See that clump of little spruces? All right—if you were a fisher, an' the hunters came up on the east side o' the thicket an' made a big noise, thrashing an' hollering, what would you do?"

"I get you," Lindsay grinned. "Suppose you'll want to do the shooting, 'long as it's your idea. All right —go get in your place. I'll be the big noise."

"Remember," Jim warned him as they parted; "he's tired. Maybe he won't budge at first. Don't get discouraged. Just keep at it and make him think you're sure coming right in after him!"

Jim took his stand about fifteen yards from the west side of the brush pile, half hidden by a tree trunk and looking down his rifle barrel at the place where the fisher ought to appear. There was a wait of several seconds, then a sudden uproar broke loose on the opposite side of the thicket. Intent as he was on getting a possible sight of the game he had trailed so far, Jim couldn't repress a chuckle at the riot his brother was raising. It began with blood-curdling yells and a crashing in the brush that sounded like a tree falling. The whooping and smashing of sticks continued for half a minute with scarcely an interruption. Then silence.

Jim's finger was curled on the trigger, tense with impatience. What was the matter with that guy? Hadn't he told him to keep on making a noise until—

Crack! Over beyond the thicket Lindsay's rifle broke the quiet. "Hey!" came the boy's excited shout.

[191]

"By golly, I got him!"

With a slightly let-down feeling, Jim tramped around the tangle of brush and looked for his brother.

"Over here!" Lindsay called. "He tried to put one over on us. Skipped out the south side, the way he came in. I'd left my gun against a tree an' had to grab it an' take a quick shot. Look!" he held the animal up gloatingly. "Got him through the head an' didn't spoil the skin!"

It was a big male fisher, thin and bony but in excellent fur.

"Pretty shooting," Jim admitted, not without envy. "He ought to be worth sixty dollars. That's not bad wages, even for three days' work!"

They settled their packs and hiked back to the river. It was no use trying to make Wababimiga that night, Jim decided. The day was half gone and there were twenty-five miles of heavy breaking between them and the family's camp. They plodded wearily up the stream, looking at Jim's cubbies as they went. At the foot of Porcupine Lake Lindsay found a big snowshoe rabbit in one of the traps.

"Of course there's not much meat on him," he said, picking up the frozen body. "Still, with two more meals to eat, we'll need all the grub we can find."

They spent the night in Jim's cabin on the lake. Rabbit stew made them a sparse supper, and in their packs they found enough tea and bread crusts to piece out a skimpy breakfast. When the last crumb was eaten they tightened their belts and set out through a gently falling snow for Waba.

It was a hungry pair of boys that hurried along the last few miles of trail to the home cabin that afternoon.

"Gosh!" Lindsay growled. "Seems as if I could chew up an old boot an' like it!"

"Yeah?" replied Jim. "Well, you can have your old boot. Me—I'll take a big mess of fried moose meat an' mashed potatoes an' hot biscuits an' maple syrup."

"Stop it!" moaned the younger boy. "You're breaking my heart! An' besides, you didn't put in deep-dish apple pie."

Seven or eight inches of new snow had fallen when they finally reached home shortly before dark. The woodpiles and dog kennels were blurry mounds of white, and the path to the shed door, shoveled out by the girls, was a narrow trench between six-foot walls of snow.

Mrs. Vanderbeck heard them taking off their snow-shoes in the shed and opened the door to peer out. "Well, I declare!" she cried. "So you did get here at last. We thought you'd given up an' gone back to your traps. Got away, did he?"

Lindsay pulled the fisher out of his pack-sack and held it up for her inspection. "Doesn't look like it, does it?" he said with pride. "But Ma; Listen—is supper 'most ready? We haven't tasted Christian food since yesterday morning!"

The good woman flung up her hands in horror. "You come right inside," she said. "Get your things off an' I'll have your supper on the table in five minutes. My land! You poor youngsters!"

She bustled back to the stove and soon had great platters of food in front of the famished pair. They ate till they could hold no more and then sat back to give the family a detailed account of the three-day hunt.

Big Lindsay chuckled when they came to Jim's stratagem for getting the fisher out of the brush heap. "That's the way it always works," he said. "You try to think like an animal would an' you'll find they're about two jumps ahead of you every time. It's lucky Lindsay happened to see him when he ducked out."

*   *   *   *

The boys spent another day at Waba before starting back to the Squaw. They cut and hauled half a dozen sled-loads of firewood, dug out the sawhorse and sawed up the logs in stove lengths. Meanwhile their mother baked loaf after brown loaf of bread. She meant, she said, to make it up to them for their recent fast.

On the morning of the 11th of February, Jim,

Lindsay and Ida harnessed one team of dogs and took the trail north toward Porcupine Lake. They had the sled loaded with their duffel and with all the fresh-baked bread they could stow aboard. The snow was too deep to move fast, but they reached Jim's home camp with half an hour of daylight to spare.

It was warm that night and a light rain made slush on the river. Jim and Lindsay, who had planned a trip together down the Squaw, decided it was useless to take the dogs. "From now on," Jim said, "it's likely to keep thawing and freezing right along. You can't use dogs when the slush balls up their feet. Ida can take the team back to Waba, and we'll pack our own duffel."

Their sister got breakfast for them and helped them fill their knapsacks. Then the dogs were harnessed and she departed on the southbound trail. The boys put on their snowshoes, swung up their packs and started down the river. The surface had settled after the thaw, and was fairly firm. They had painted their snowshoes with a concoction brewed from alder bark, which prevented the slush from sticking to the frames and woven thongs. Thus they were able to go ahead at a good pace in spite of the loads they carried.

Jim dug out his trap-houses along the way and was pleased to find one belated mink to add to his catch of fur. On the river, a little way above the long carry, they sighted a huge old bull moose feeding in the

[195]

alders. He had shed his antlers, but his great size and the pendulous "bell" under his throat made it obvious that he was a patriarch.

Half a mile farther on they saw more moose—three of them together, this time—wading through the sodden snow. A small bull led the group and a cow with a half-grown calf accompanied him.

"Look!" said Lindsay. "Funny thing—that one's still wearing his horns."

"Sure," Jim answered. "He's only got about a two-foot spread. Light little horns like that don't fall off as easy as the big ones. He probably won't shed for another month."

They spent the night at the Long Portage lean-to and went on next day to Jim's lower camp without stopping at Beaver Lake. The only fur they found in the traps was a mink, and that had to be thrown away. It was buried so deep under snow and ice that Jim cut the skin with the ax in getting it out. Also mice had been gnawing at the hide and several patches of fur were destroyed.

When they reached the place where the cabin ought to be, Jim looked around in consternation. He thought he knew every bush and tree and bend in the river by now, but where was his camp?

At last, walking closer on top of the drifts, he saw a small, dark triangle under a mound of snow. A little area of logs below the peak of the ridgepole was all that showed. The rest of the shack was completely engulfed in white.

Tired and hungry, the boys set to work laboriously and dug the snow away from the door. It was pitch-dark before they got the cabin warm and their supper cooked.

"Tell you what," said Jim, as he lay back resting after the meal was finished, "I think I'll pick up the traps, down this way. There'll be mighty little fur after the middle of February, and it's too much work to make it pay. There's only two weeks left of the season any way."

Lindsay agreed with him. Next morning they went on down the river, springing and taking up such traps as Jim had set below the camp.

It was snowing lightly when they returned to Long Portage, the following day. On the trip up river they had picked up all the traps, including those at Beaver Lake, and they came staggering into camp heavily laden with clanking steel. "The Chain Gang," Lindsay called them. "Guess I don't want to be a convict after all," he jested pantingly, as he flung down his load on the cabin floor.

Jim looked out before bedtime to see what the weather promised. The snow had stopped again and a few stars were struggling through the clouds. It was warm outside. Barely below freezing, he thought. As he started to close the door a faint, shivery sound came through the night.

"Wolves are out," he remarked, dropping the door-latch in place. "Sounds like a pack of 'em, off to the south somewhere."

Half a dozen times in the night he woke to hear that wild, eerie music, never very near, but coming, it seemed, from every point of the compass.

Breaking trail next day on the stretch of river between the long carry and Jim's home camp, the boys watched for wolf tracks.

"Funny thing," said Lindsay, when they had covered several miles. "I'd have sworn I heard 'em somewhere up this way."

"Me, too," Jim replied. "You can't be sure, though. Unless you're outdoors it's hard to tell just where a wolf's howl comes from. Dad told me once they have a trick to the way they throw the sound. That's to fool the game, I guess. Say—look at that! There's one thing they didn't kill, last night!"

A gaunt brown cow moose was wading knee deep in the snow close to the bank. And even as they watched, a pair of twin calves stepped out from behind her, cocking their ridiculous great ears in the boys' direction.

That afternoon they took three ermine out of the cubbies, and as they neared the camp, Jim found a live lynx, caught by the toes of its hind foot in a No. 2 mink trap.

"It's a good thing these cats are dumb," he told Lindsay, when he had shot it. "One good pull and his paw would have come out clean as a whistle."

After a night in Jim's camp, where they refilled their pack-sacks with supplies, the boys set out next day for Lindsay's line, cutting north through the woods to Abosabi Lake. The younger boy had traps set all along the chain of ponds—Abosabi, Loon and Sucker Lake—and by dint of steady work they came out on Squaw Lake by nightfall. One mink was all the fur they found, but the day was enlivened by the sight of a pair of caribou galloping through deep snow on Sucker Lake. Lindsay was walking in the lead as they came down the thoroughfare toward Squaw Lake, a mile from camp. Suddenly Jim saw him disappear. Running forward he found the boy trying to pull himself out of an air hole through which he had dropped without warning. He threw himself flat on the crust and pushed his snowshoes forward, giving his brother something to hold on to. In a moment he had him out.

Lindsay was between rage and laughter. "Darn brook was only a couple o' feet deep, down under there. Wet me to my knees," he said. "But that sure is a helpless feeling when you start to fall!"

Fortunately the temperature was not very low. They hustled on to Lindsay's Squaw Lake camp and got a fire started before the youngster's toes had time to freeze.

The morning of the 18th broke clear and cold, a good day for travel. When the boys had followed Lindsay's trap-line a few miles down the Squaw they swung to the right on an overland trail through the bush. At noon they struck Jim's route from Porcupine Lake to Waba, and before sunset the family's cabin was in sight.

Mrs. Vanderbeck was the only one there to greet them. Big Lindsay and the girls were off on a trip to Nakina for supplies.

Jim stretched his legs luxuriously under the big puncheon table. "Well, kid," he told his brother, as they settled down to a meal of their mother's cooking, "let's see how much we can get done before they come back. There's the spring wood to cut, an' nets to pull, an' a couple o' moose hides to fit up into snowshoe filling, and Dad's traps to tend, an'—"

"Hey!" mumbled Lindsay, his mouth full of hot biscuit, "quit talkin' about work an' let me enjoy this supper!"

Lynx

XVIII

In the morning the work got under way in earnest. There was a fish net staked out a few hundred yards from the camp landing. When they had sawed and split enough wood to last their mother several days, the boys started shoveling snow away from the net poles. The catch was only nine fish. However, two of them were "snakes"—great northern pike that weighed thirty or forty pounds apiece.

The next two days they spent in following their father's trap-lines, first to the south and east, then westward, to the head of the lake. The weather had been steadily cold and there was a good crust, so it was possible to use a dog sled.

"Whose team'll we take—yours or mine?" Lindsay

asked, as they laid out the harness.

"Neither one," Jim replied. "Not for working up the Lake, any way. We'll want that old husky of Dad's for a leader because he knows the cubbies better'n we do. My Paddy'll pull behind him, an' we can take one o' your dogs for the third one."

The makeshift team worked well together after one or two quarrels. It was a big help, as Jim had foreseen, to have at the head of the team a dog who was familiar with the location of the traps. Any good leader will stop at each cubby in turn, once he has been over the line a few times.

They found no fur in any of the traps, and the weather grew steadily colder. By the end of the second day the temperature had dropped to a point where it was hard to keep the dogs moving. They made camp in their father's cabin at the head of Wababimiga and a roaring fire of logs in the stove kept them fairly comfortable that night. The next morning was one of the coldest of the winter. They had no thermometer, but Jim knew, the moment he felt the breath freeze on the fur of his hood, that the dogs would never go on such a day.

They ate breakfast and waited for the sun to get up, in hopes it would moderate. Finally Jim took his ax and went over to the fish net. He cut one pole out, after an hour's labor, and was starting toward the other when he realized there was no feeling left in his face. He stopped quickly, chafing one cheek with his mitten. Numb! He left the pole on the ice and started back to the cabin at a run.

There was some loose snow under a hole in the crust by the door. Jim picked up a double handful and began to rub it on both cheeks. Slowly a burning sensation came under the skin. A fierce, biting pain tortured his face. Only then did he stop chafing the frozen skin and go inside the cabin.

Lindsay looked up from getting lunch. "Frostbite?" he asked. "Here, don't come anywhere near the stove. Better keep over there by the door till the ache goes out o' your face."

They stayed in camp the rest of the day. With somewhat more warmth in the air next morning they were able to pull the net and pack a dozen more fish on the sled. Then Lindsay took the trail down the lake with the dogs, while Jim swung north. He wanted to get over an outlying line of his father's that ran overland across the hills.

He tramped along through the open birch and poplar growth, enjoying the winter sunshine. None of the traps held any fur, but he saw several moose. One was a small calf, strayed from its mother. It was so frightened and confused at Jim's approach that it went tearing up an almost perpendicular hillside,

[203]

missed its footing, and tumbled half way to the bottom again before getting its awkward legs untangled.

Jim reached the home cabin at five o'clock that night. He had passed Joe Leake's shack at dusk, wading through a great pile of scraped moose hair that lay on top of the snow like a tumbled haystack. It made him almost physically sick to figure the number of moose that must have been slaughtered by the Cree that winter. Some of the Indian's dogs yelped at him as he went past, but the cabin door was not opened, and he hurried on without stopping.

Lindsay had reached home before him and was reading a book by the lamp when Jim stamped in. The older boy was tired and gruff. "That all you've got to do?" he asked. "I thought, with all afternoon at home, you'd have the *babiche* 'most made!"

"Huh!" grunted Lindsay. "I only came in an hour ago. Lead dog went lame, half way down the lake, an' I made slow time. Besides, Ma says Dad an' the girls won't be home till Sunday, so we've got a couple o' days to cut hides."

Babiche is the Indian name for snowshoe filler. It has to be made each winter in large enough quantities to fill all the frames used by a family, for daily use over all kinds of surfaces wears out the woven thongs. Jim had learned the art from his Ojibway friends, the

Lagarde boys.

Before breakfast he went out to the shed and brought in the frozen hide of one of the young bulls they had killed in the autumn. He laid the stiff skin on the rack of poles above the stove and left it there for a couple of hours, while he and Lindsay ate their morning meal and did the chores. Then, when the hide had thawed out and become flexible, he draped it over a slanting pole, set up in the yard. In a temperature of 20 or more below zero it soon began to stiffen again. While the hide was freezing, the boys searched in the shed for the upper foreleg bone of a moose, saved for the purpose. This they split lengthwise with an ax, so that the edges of the bone had an almost razor-like sharpness.

Now began the hardest part of the job. Jim held the ends of the bone knife in both hands and pulled it toward him over the surface of the hide, like a draw-shave. The coarse, gray-brown hairs were cut away cleanly, leaving hardly a sign of stubble on the frozen skin. Every few moments the edge of the bone grew dull and had to be trimmed sharp again with a hunting knife.

When all the hair had been removed, the hide was thawed out again and sewn into a big wooden frame, six feet square. Then they placed it outside to freeze once more. It was midafternoon before it had frozen hard enough for the second scraping. Jim whetted an ax until the blade was almost keen enough to split a hair. It had to be handled skilfully to avoid cutting gashes in the skin. Holding the head of the ax in one hand and the helve in the other, he began scraping the boardlike hide. First the outer layer of skin was cut away, right down to the roots of the hair. Then the inner surface was likewise scraped clean. What remained was the toughest part of the hide, an eighth of an inch thick.

That night they took the skin out of its frame and cut it into long, even strips, about the width of Jim's little finger. When it was wet and stretched it would become much narrower, but for the time being it was finished *babiche*.

The second hide was prepared and cut up the following day, and by nightfall they had enough rawhide strips to fill all the snowshoes they owned. Sunday, as always at Wababimiga, was a day of rest. The boys took baths, helped their mother with the cooking, and spent the rest of the time reading. Big Lindsay and the girls arrived that afternoon, rosy and hungry from their journey down the lake.

"Well, boys," said their father, when the evening lamp was lit, "season's about over. Two more days left in February, so we'll all have to start springin' traps tomorrow. We've done fairly well, amongst us, this winter. If we have a good muskrat season we'll make

[206]

out fine. I heard in Nakina that rats'll bring a dollar
an' a quarter, this year."

*   *   *   *

Since Jim had already sprung the traps on about
half his lines, he waited over a day to take up his
father's traps along the north shore of Wababimiga.
The following morning—the last of February—he
got an early start for the Squaw. It had stayed cold
and the going was fast on the well-broken trail. He
used his own team of Bruno and Pat, both fat and
strong from their long rest. By the time he reached
his home camp that night he had half a sled-load of
traps taken from the Porcupine Lake line, and there
were a mink and two ermine to add to his store of fur.

He routed the team out at three o'clock next morning and mushed down the river, collecting traps as
he went. It rained a little and the warm weather made
the going soft in the afternoon. For the next two days
he had to do all his work in the early morning, before
the slush could thaw.

It was when he was approaching his home camp,
the last morning of the trip, that he saw two good-
sized timber wolves come out of the bush ahead of
him. The dogs stopped in their tracks, silent but uneasy, and watched the big gray beasts trot out on the
ice, not fifty yards away. Jim hurried back to the
sled. Foolishly he had piled traps on top of his rifle,

which lay in its deerskin cover near the middle of the toboggan. With one eye on the wolves he tried to get the gun out without upsetting the load of traps.

They stood there watching him until the moment he succeeded in pulling the rifle free. Then both turned and made for the woods at an easy lope. They timed their exit so perfectly that he had barely whipped the stock to his shoulder when they disappeared.

"Not very smart," he growled to himself. "Not smart enough for those babies any way. They just stood and grinned till the gun came in sight."

For the rest of that journey he carried the rifle in the crook of his arm.

Lindsay was waiting for him at the cabin. The boy had finished picking up his own traps the day before and come down river that morning. Between them they had four mink to wind up the winter season. They skinned them that afternoon and were ready for bed by sundown.

Traveling with the dogs at this time of year meant a definite change of schedule. They moved well enough while the surface of the snow was frozen, but by noon each day the sun was likely to make the going sticky. Consequently the boys kept much the same hours as a city milkman. They rose long before dawn and went to bed about five or five-thirty.

Getting up at three, they made the run to Waba over the crust next morning. That was the fourth of

March. That afternoon and the next three days they spent cutting and hauling the spring's wood. On the eighth, with three teams of dogs, the whole family except Mrs. Vanderbeck made an early start for Nakina.

They knew the fur buyer was to be in town that day, and so they went straight through without a stop. On the level crust the girls and Big Lindsay were able to ride the sleds part of the time, but for Jim and his brother the trip was thirty-five miles of steady hiking.

When they reached the village, an hour after sunset, they discovered how fortunate this forced march had been. The buyer was leaving on the morning train, and a delay would have cost them a chance to dispose of their furs. As it was, the combined catch of the family was sold for a little over $350. They were able to send off an order for supplies on the same train that carried the shrewd old fur merchant back to civilization.

The boys enjoyed the luxury of lying abed till nine o'clock next morning, and what was left of the day they spent resting and visiting their friends in town. But on the tenth they had to get to work again. There was a small log ice house in the rear of their home at Nakina, and a few hundred yards away, down the hill, there was a pond of clear water.

At breakfast that morning Big Lindsay cocked a

quizzical eyebrow at his sons. "Seems to me I re-
collect you fellers like ice cream for Sunday dinner
in the summertime," he remarked. "Guess maybe
we'd better get that ice house filled up."

Going at the job with a will, the boys soon had the
snow cleared off an area of the pond twenty or thirty
feet square. Then they chopped a hole through the
ice and went to work with a big saw. When the ice
had been cut into cubes, two feet on a side and about
the same in thickness, each block had to be lifted out
of the water and pulled up the hill on a sled. It took
the next two days to finish stacking it in the ice
house. Then another day was spent hauling sawdust
from town to pack around the ice.

The dogs got plenty of work that week, for no
sooner was the ice house filled than they had to start
hauling in wood for the summer.

On March 16, the provisions they had ordered from
Port Arthur arrived at the freight station. That was
the signal for still more concentrated labor. The
supplies were brought over to the storehouse and
sorted into a number of sled-loads, each to be taken
to a different line camp for the spring rat-trapping.

Jim and Lindsay were the first to start back into
the bush. They got away at dawn, their sleds piled
with potatoes, carefully wrapped in blankets and
tarpaulins. A quick run brought them to Poplar Lake,
and they stopped at Lindsay's camp, for there was

danger of freezing their precious cargo if they went too far. At noon next day they pulled in at the Waba cabin with the potatoes still in good shape.

Things had been happening in their absence, they found. Over in a corner of the warm room lay Blackie, the female husky, left behind when the other dogs made the trip to Nakina. She growled at the boys but made no move to rise.

"Hey, Ma," cried Lindsay, pulling off his parka, "what's ol' Blackie doin' in the house? It's bad for sled dogs, Dad says—"

Mrs. Vanderbeck chuckled. "Hush boy," she said, "an' don't go off half cocked. She's got as much right here as you have. Look at this!"

In a box under the edge of the pole bed were five squirming bits of black and gray fur.

"Sure," said Jim. "Didn't you know she was goin' to have 'em? Say, they're whoppers, too! Big an' handsome. How many he-ones in the litter, Ma?"

"Three," she replied. "I s'pose that's all we'll keep. Too bad, when they're all doing so fine."

On the 19th the boys were up and away by four in the morning. The frozen trail was fast and they rode the sleds all the way to town, making the journey in less than six hours.

"Not bad, with only two dogs to a sled," Jim commented. "Of course, Emile did it last winter in three hours an' fifty minutes, but those four police dogs of his are practically a racing team."

There was a day's delay in Nakina for one or two more purchases to arrive. It was the warmest day they had had. Melting snow made a steady drip from the eaves and the sun blazed down on pools of water in the road behind the station. When the whole Vanderbeck clan started for Wababimiga next morning the temperature was still above freezing.

"Take it careful, boys," warned Big Lindsay. "The ice won't be so solid on the streams after a thaw like this."

Jim nodded and led off down the trail to Cordingley Lake. On his toboggan, in addition to his own duffel, were two five-gallon cans of gasoline. It would be used in the outboard motor later in the spring, when the lakes opened up.

The boy was proud of his team. He knew old Bruno, with the sturdy Pat behind him, could outpull any of the other pairs, and once they were out on the lake he lengthened his stride. When he rounded the first bend of Cranberry River the rest of the convoy was out of sight, half a mile behind.

Then, without the slightest warning, came catastrophe. One moment Jim was hiking along down the middle of the river, humming a song. The next found him plunged over his head in icy water. A patch of rotten ice had given under his weight and left him fighting for his life in the swift-moving current.

Otter

XIX

THE gap in the ice through which Jim had fallen
was hardly bigger than the area his snowshoes had
covered—six or seven feet long and less than half
as wide. He got his head above water and clutched
frantically at the broken edges of the hole, trying
to pull himself out. It was hopeless. He might easily
have lifted his weight alone, but the current tugged
mercilessly at the snowshoes, still fast to his feet. He
knew that if he lost his grip even for an instant he
would be dragged under the ice.

A dozen yards away was the sled, the dogs sitting
in their harness, staring at him uneasily.

"Bruno!" he called. "Come here, boy!"

The old lead dog whimpered and sprang forward,
but Pat hung back, snarling. He was afraid to come
nearer that treacherous chasm in the ice. Like a gray
tornado the police dog whirled on his team-mate,

chopping at his shoulder with wicked white fangs.

Jim's head was pulled under momentarily, and when he came up again he was half strangled, desperate. His numb hands were slipping. He was through, unless something happened pretty quick. It did. Crawling on his belly along the ice came Bruno, dragging the other dog and the loaded sled after him.

"Come boy—come on!" gasped Jim, in a choking whisper.

The grizzled leader wriggled nearer—nearer—till one of Jim's clutching hands could seize the harness. As he flung his weight on the edge of the hole the ice cracked ominously. Bruno whined and trembled but stayed where he was, and Jim slipped back, afraid of pulling the dogs down with him. He must find some other way. If only he had a long plank—the toboggan!

In another instant he was hauling in the trace strap, hand over hand. He reached Paddy's collar and pulled the struggling dog past. Slowly he was dragging the long sled closer. At last his hands were on the lashings at the tail of the toboggan. He wrapped his numb wrists in the heavy cord and put all the breath he had left into a despairing yell.

"Hi, now! Mush, Bruno! Mush, Pat!"

The thongs strained at his hands. The sled jerked forward away from the hole. He felt the ice crack and rumble under his body but the dogs kept moving.

Ten seconds later he was lying on the solid surface, exhausted but safe.

"Holy smoke!" he shivered, clambering up on shaky knees. "That was close—too close!"

When the rest of the party came around the bend, they found the boy crouched above a roaring fire on the bank of the stream.

"Keep over this side—away from that rotten ice," he yelled to them. And when they had gathered around his steaming person he told briefly, and somewhat sheepishly, what had happened.

"Go ahead, Dad," he grinned, at the end. "Go ahead an' say it. I've got it comin' to me!"

But Big Lindsay had Bruno's head between his knees. He made only one remark. "I wouldn't take ten fisher skins for this feller," he said.

*　　*　　*　　*

The next two days at Waba were merry ones. With the whole family together in the cozy cabin, the walls echoed all day with songs and laughter. The weather had turned colder, with snow squalls blowing. Not much could be done outdoors. The dogs had a well-earned rest after their weeks of heavy pulling, and the boys stayed inside, mending clothes and moccasins, reading and playing games.

The husky pups were thriving. Though they and their mother had now been put back in one of the outdoor kennels, Jim brought the little fellows in for an hour or two on the second day of the storm. They tumbled about the puncheon floor, barking in tiny, ferocious squeaks at the dignified old tabby cat.

The third morning there was nearly two feet of new snow on the ground. It had turned to a drizzle of rain in the night and the surface was water soaked and heavy.

"Can't use the sleds today," Big Lindsay said at breakfast. "Got to put in time some way, though. How about makin' some snowshoe bows, Jim? S'pose you could locate a good birch?"

Jim thought a minute. "Yes," he answered. "I remember spotting one that would do fine. It was down Waba River. Good an' straight, an' growing close to water. I'll go down right away an' see if I can find it."

Before starting, the boy rubbed his snowshoes with alder bark "soup" to keep them from sticking in the wet snow. Then he took his ax and set out. It was not more than three miles overland to the river and, in spite of the heavy breaking, he made it in a little over an hour. A five-minute search brought him to the slim young birch by the bank. It was a perfect tree for his purpose. Straight as a plumb-line and eight inches thick at the base.

Jim braced his feet and drew back the ax for the first blow. Before he had time to deliver it, a shadow of black wings beat by overhead and he heard the hoarse croak of a raven. The boy paused, watching the big bird flap and circle above the trees a scant hundred yards away. Something must be dead or dying there. Maybe an animal caught in a trap. At any rate, his curiosity had to be satisfied.

He laid the ax down by the tree and went quietly downstream toward the place where the raven was hovering and cawing. The wind was from the east, blowing into his face. As he rounded a thick clump of young spruce the breeze brought a sound to his ears —a low, intermittent, snarling that seemed to come from more than one throat.

He moved still more carefully, peering ahead through the dense brush. Then he saw them—big, gray-white shapes moving in a closely huddled mass. Between them and under them he could catch fleeting glimpses of ruddy brown and an occasional flash of crimson. A pack of timber wolves tearing at the body of a slain deer!

He was silently raving at himself for neglecting to bring a rifle, when something warned the animals that an enemy was near. Perhaps a flaw in the wind had let his scent drift through. In an instant the pack was in flight. Four—five—six of them—floundering away through the heavy snow.

The boy turned and fairly ran back to his birch. A dozen quick strokes of the ax brought it down. He trimmed away the branches, cut off a ten-foot butt stick, and swung it over his shoulder.

The log was heavy but his big winter snowshoes bore up well in the packed snow. He went back to camp even faster than he had come.

"Here y'are, Dad," he panted, as he flung the birch down in the shed. "Where's Lindsay? Where's my rifle? Bunch o' wolves back there! In this wet snow we've got a swell chance to catch up with 'em!"

His brother heard him and came on the run. He was already dressed for outdoors. "Here!" he said. "I've got the guns an' a pocketful of extra cartridges. Let's go!"

"Wait a minute, now," Big Lindsay interrupted. "Those wolves'll keep. Don't rush off without any packs or you'll both be sorry. No tellin' but you may have to sleep out."

With the girls' help, they hastily packed their knapsacks and rolled up a couple of blankets and a tarpaulin apiece.

It still lacked an hour of noon when they reached the river and passed the stump of Jim's birch tree.

"Easy now," whispered the older boy. "They might have come back after I left."

But when they came in sight of the dead deer they saw only a pair of ravens that flapped hurriedly away.

"All right," Jim said. "If the pack kept together, they'll be easy to follow."

The trail of the wolves led away southward through

thickly wooded country. The difficulty they had had in running in the heavy snow was apparent from the deep, wallowing track they left. At first there were several yards between the depressions that marked their jumps. Then the distance shortened, and the tracks drew together into a single narrow path, packed down to a foot or more below the surface.

The boys plodded along in silence, their eyes intent on the trail ahead. Once they found a place where the wolves had stopped to rest. Two or three of them had lain down and left the mark of their curled up bodies in the lee of a jack-pine clump.

"Probably didn't stop here long," Jim said. "They were gone before they got wind of us. See—they weren't running as if they were scared."

The ground had become gradually lower as they neared the muskeg country. There were fewer trees, and most of the growth was tamarack—mournful, moss-bearded poles rising out of the boggy waste.

"You gettin' hungry?" Jim asked, when the sun had begun to sink toward the southwest.

"Not a mite," Lindsay answered stoutly. "Come on—we ought to be catchin' up on these babies by now."

They quickened their stride and pushed on, mile after mile, into the muskeg. The wind had gone down, but what little there was still blew into their faces. It stirred the boughs of a low, dense rabbit-bush ahead.

Jim stopped and motioned to Lindsay with his hand.

"Look," he whispered. "The trail goes right into that patch of bush. If they're still in there they'll see us in a minute, an' make a break on the other side. We've got to circle it an' keep hid if we can. You go that way. I'll sneak around this end."

As they separated Jim realized that his own course, to the left, would take him to windward of the thicket. That meant that anything hiding in the bush would catch his scent first. Lindsay ought to get a shot.

He crouched low, to keep out of sight, and moved quietly along behind a screen of scrub spruce and tamarack. He had made something over half the circuit of the rabbit-bush when there was a sudden yell from Lindsay, followed in the same second by the report of a rifle.

Jim leaped out into the open, the Winchester springing to his shoulder. Sixty or seventy yards away, on the south side of the thicket, the wolves had broken cover and were wallowing through the snow. Jim swung the muzzle of his rifle, leading the nearest of the gray killers by a foot or two. His bullet passed over the wolf's head and raised a cloud of snow beyond. The second shot was lower, but it stopped the beast only for a second. He fired again, apparently without effect, and the next moment the pack had disappeared among the trees.

"Come on!" Jim shouted. "I think I hit one!"

"So did I," came Lindsay's response. "Here he is, dead as a door-nail!"

Jim ran over to the edge of the thicket where he saw his brother stooping over a furry gray mass in the snow.

"I'd been a pretty poor shot if I missed this one," chuckled Lindsay. "He came out on my side, headin' right toward me. Turned just before I fired an' I drilled him back of the shoulder. Heart, I guess. He didn't make but one more jump."

"He's dead, all right," said Jim. "Let's leave him an' keep after the others. Mine couldn't have got very far."

He refilled the magazine of his rifle and they took up the chase again. There were flecks of red in the trail close to the woods. Seeing them, the boys quickened their pace to a run.

"Bet we find him inside of half a mile," Jim panted.

But he would have lost that bet. They followed the crimson-stained track for an hour—two hours— and the sun was a red disk on the horizon.

Jim paused to wipe his damp forehead with his sleeve. "Beats me!" he growled. "He must have lost a gallon o' blood, by now. You'd think—"

"Look!" cried Lindsay, and pointed to a tangle of brush just ahead. There was a half-hidden movement among the dead boughs. Then Jim saw a gray

[221]

head and a sagging, weary body emerge from the thicket. He raised his rifle and sent a bullet crashing through the wolf's brain.

The boys bent over their victim and marveled. The whole left shoulder bone had been crushed and mangled by Jim's earlier shot. And as if that were not enough, the wet snow had matted in great icy lumps on the fur of the wolf's belly and hindquarters.

"He must have been draggin' ten pounds of extra weight," said Lindsay, "an' he came seven or eight miles with one leg clean out o' commission! Gosh!"

"Well, it's sunset," said Jim, looking around him, "and we're a good twenty miles from home. Dad knew something when he told us to carry packs. This muskeg isn't the swellest place in the world for an open camp, but I guess we'll make out well enough."

They dragged the body of the wolf back as far as the first clump of spruce and put up a makeshift shelter of poles and boughs. When the fire was going and Lindsay had started the supper, Jim set about skinning his trophy.

"Makes a nice pelt," he yawned at length, holding up the huge gray hide. "That'll buy a lot of salt an' tea an' cartridges. Boy, I'm tired! Let's find out how those beds feel."

*　　　*　　　*　　　*

A sharp chill in the air woke them before dawn. The thaw had ended in the night and the snow was frozen in a solid crust that made the return trip easier. They found Lindsay's wolf undisturbed and stopped long enough to skin it. Then, with the two pelts rolled up on top of their packs, they followed their back track to the river and home. It was midafternoon when they came in sight of the cabin and heard Ida's welcoming hail.

"Got 'em, did you?" their father beamed from the shed door. "Well, you made better'n day's wages on that trip. It always does my heart good to see a wolf put out o' business. They kill more game than all the hunters in Canada."

He had made a good start on the snowshoe frames and Jim helped him finish them the next day. It was a job that took some skill. When the log had been carefully split lengthwise into billets, each piece was worked down to the proper size and smoothness with a knife. Then the straight-grained sticks were steamed until they were pliable and bent into curves over a form. Finally the cross-braces were mortised in, and the toes and tails fastened together with rawhide thongs. With the bows finished, all that remained was to weave in the filler—a task that the women folks could help with in the evenings.

Jim went back to cutting wood with Lindsay the

next morning, and the two boys chopped and sawed to such good effect that in two days they had enough fuel to last out the spring.

The 28th of March came in clear and cold—a good day to travel with the dogs. Big Lindsay called the boys at sunrise.

"Time to move the canoes, an' get 'em in place for the spring's trapping," he told them. "There's ten canoes in all, an' some are already racked up where we'll use 'em. The others ought to be hauled now, so they'll be on the spot when the ice starts to go."

XX

THE canoe-sleds had been stacked at the rear of the cabin all winter. They consisted of a pair of curved wooden runners with two cross blocks and a padded "bunk" on which to lay the canoe. They were fastened trailer-wise to the tail of a regular dog sled. The nose of the craft rested on a roll of canvas tied across the back of the toboggan, and the stern stuck out a few feet beyond the runners of the trailer. When all was lashed firmly in place it was possible to carry a canoe over the roughest trails without damaging it.

Four of the ten canoes were to be left at different points around Wababimiga for their father's use. The other six they divided equally between their own territories.

With smooth glare ice on the lakes the hauling was

comparatively easy. The boys spent that night in the log shack at the head of Waba. Next day they journeyed to Porcupine Lake and brought back a canoe that had been left there in the fall. And on the 30th with all four boats in place at the home lake, they set out, each by a different route, to his own ground.

Jim found the going soft on the trail to Squaw Lake. It was warm and wet in the afternoon and the dogs had to stop often to rest. He made camp in the cabin at the foot of the lake and went on down the river in the morning.

There was open water at many of the rapids, so that he had to cut detours through the bush. The seven miles to his winter home camp took him the best part of four hours. He loaded one of the two canoes he had stored there and returned to Squaw Lake by sundown. This cabin, which had served Lindsay as a line camp through the winter, was to be Jim's headquarters for the muskrat season.

An excerpt from his diary for the next day reads as follows:

"*April* 1. Go down river for another canoe. No April fools for me this year, I said to myself as I walked along. Almost immediately the ice went out from under me and down I went up to my middle. The two dogs were lucky. Well, you can never tell. It was a warm day so the water soon ran out of my clothes and I got my other canoe and started back up. When I got to camp I changed my clothes. Very many mink tracks along bank and I saw two of them. Always the way. You see more fur out of season than you do in."

The next two days he hauled one canoe to the head of Squaw Lake and another up to Sucker Lake. With a boat at each piece of open water he would be able to move about without portaging when the rat-trapping began.

On the morning of the 4th the air had such a soft, warm feel that he knew spring was really on the way. The chickadees, hopping busily through the spruce branches, had changed their song from a pert *chick-adee-dee-dee* to a wheedling cadence of two notes; *dee-dee, dee-dee*. It wouldn't be long now till the fox cubs would be playing in the sun on sandy hillsides. He looked up at the mild blue sky, half expecting to see a flock of mallards winging over. But it was still too early for ducks. They always delayed their arrival till the ponds and streams began to open.

Jim got to Lindsay's Poplar Lake camp that afternoon. The place was empty. However, by the time he had a fire lighted in the stove, a barking of dogs announced his brother's arrival. Lindsay had placed his three canoes and gone to Nakina for one of the remaining loads of provisions.

The boys spent the night there together. In the

morning Jim transferred the supplies to his own sled. He would take them on to Waba while Lindsay returned to town for another load.

Starting two hours before daybreak, as was customary on these spring journeys, Jim was over the portages and going down the long white track of Wababimiga before noon. He reached the cabin just as luncheon was being put on the table. While he ate, the girls gave him all the news. Miranda, the black fisher, had sulked and refused her food, and finally, the night before, she had dug her way out under the wire. Mrs. Vanderbeck sighed as the story was told.

"I got real attached to the pretty little thing," she said. "I'm glad she won't be turned into fur, though. Reckon she's back with her own kind by now."

The puppies were growing fast and taking on definite individualities. Big Lindsay was impatiently awaiting the day when they could be harnessed to a tiny sled and given their first introduction to the business of life. He already had a leader picked.

"That gray feller," he chuckled, "is the born boss o' the litter. He won't take any sass from the others unless they both gang him at once."

But the thing that made Mary and Ida most excited was the view they had had that morning of five caribou on the lake. The herd had come out of the woods to the north and trotted right across the cove. "So close," Ida exclaimed, "that I could have hit 'em

[228]

with a snowball!"

Jim feigned astonishment. "Why—they must've been right on the front porch!" he said, and ducked hastily to avoid his sister's wrath.

He did a few chores around camp that afternoon, and the next day he went with Big Lindsay to bring in birch for more snowshoe bows. The morning of the seventh he hitched up the dogs for a trip to Nakina after his spring supplies.

"Take a look in the cellar while you're there," was his father's parting injunction. "Those potatoes are likely startin' to sprout."

The boy did not finish breakfast till after daybreak, and by the time he reached Cranberry River the noon sun had softened the snow. Except on the portages he had ridden the toboggan all morning. Now, in the heavy going, he had to walk. He got to town about sundown and found Lindsay at the house, cooking supper.

"About time you showed up," grinned the younger brother. "I was down in the potato bin this mornin' and oh, boy—what a job we've got ahead of us!"

The cellar where the Vanderbeck's stored their vegetables was deep, dark and narrow. It held a good many bushels of potatoes, laid away in the fall for the year's consumption. Now it was half empty, but there was still little enough room for two broad shouldered youngsters to work.

They went down the next morning as soon as the breakfast dishes were washed. A candle, stuck on a piece of shingle, gave them all the light they had. Sprouting potatoes could hardly be classed as heavy labor, yet the constant stooping and the cramped quarters quickly told on them. Jim stood up after an hour of it and unbent his aching back.

"Wow!" he grinned wrily. "I'd sooner break trail after a blizzard! How 'bout you?"

They stayed with it through the morning, got themselves some lunch, and went back to sprout spuds all afternoon. Even then the job wasn't finished. They worked the best part of the following day before they stripped the last white tendril from the last potato.

Lindsay went out to stretch his legs when it was over, and came back looking disconsolate. "I found another job that needs doing," he reported. "It's so warm outside I'm afraid the snowbanks round the house'll melt into a regular lake. If that happens we'll have a cellar full o' water."

"Easy!" Jim replied. "Shovelin' snow ought to be pie for us after those spuds."

The drifts were four or five feet deep all around the log walls, and it took the boys practically all the next day to dig the wet snow away from the house. On the 11th the warm spell continued and the white blanket was melting fast. When they walked down the track to town that evening the ties were beginning to show through in many places. Jim was worried. "Can't travel while it stays like this," he told his brother. "All we can do now is hang around an' hope it freezes again before all the snow goes."

Michel Lagarde was standing on the station platform, stolidly watching the activities of the freight agent. Michel was the huskiest of all the Lagarde clan—a short, thick-set Ojibway, with a chest like a barrel and a gigantic pair of shoulders. In the Indian sports at Long Lac, the summer before, he had beaten all the other guides by packing a tump-line load of 450 pounds for half a mile.

His rocklike brown face did not change expression when the boys appeared, but there was a brightening spark in his deep-set black eyes.

"How're you, Michel?" Jim greeted him. "You thaw-bound, too?"

The Ojibway nodded. "Dogs won't go," he said. "Wait for freeze." Deliberately he got a blackened old pipe out of his pocket and filled it with coarse, rank tobacco. When he had it drawing well, he spoke again in a guttural bass. "You see 'em big wolf?"

"Why yes," Jim answered in surprise. "At least, we've seen his tracks, an' I guess I got a shot at him a month or so ago."

"He come roun' here las' night," Michel went on. "Scare devil out o' town Injuns. See his track followin' li'l boy."

Lindsay whistled. "Gosh!" he said. "That sounds like some o' the old stories Emile used to tell. Wolves that stole children from the French cabins back in Quebec. What are they goin' to do—hunt him?"

The Indian shook his head in disgust. "Not him," he said. "Dey hunt Eskimo squaw, mebbe. Joe Leake —him get cabin burn' some night."

It rained most of the next day. Jim read a magazine for a while, then flung it down restlessly and put on his slicker. "I'm goin' down the track," he told Lindsay. "See you at dinner time."

When he returned he had news. "What d' you think?" he called as he came in the door. "They've sent for the Mounted. That fellow Mike, in the station lunch room, told me. The track Indians are all excited about this witch-wolf business—gettin' ready to smoke out Joe Leake's woman, soon as the travelin' gets better. They don't say much, o' course, but the word got to the Game Warden an' he's wired for help."

There was quite a crowd assembled on the platform at train time that night. None of the track Indians were present. The only copper skins Jim saw were those of woodsmen and trappers like the Lagarde boys.

"What's up?" he asked one of his white friends—
a railroad section hand.

"Ain't you heard?" the fellow replied. "They're
expectin' a police sergeant. MacLeish, I think his name
is. Big feller. Six-foot-six, they say."

"Sure—I remember him!" Jim exclaimed. "He was
here three years ago, when that French trapper went
crazy an' killed a man, up on the Kowkash. Big? I'll
say he is!"

The Limited was half an hour late because of the
rains. When it finally clanked to a stop there was a
hush on the platform. The lights from warm, cozy
sleeping cars glinted on the wet rails. In the diner
there was a gleam of silver and glass, and they could
see the bored faces of well-fed city people staring out
at the dark huddle of the settlement.

In the door of one of the cars a tall, straight figure
appeared, and booted feet tramped down the steps.
Sergeant MacLeish was in the winter uniform of the
Royal Canadian Mounted, the long, dark overcoat
hiding his scarlet jacket. His face was keen and rugged, his mouth hard set. The breadth of his shoulders
and his erect, easy carriage made his height less noticeable, but he towered a full head above most of
the men around him as he strode into the station.

"Well," said Jim, as he bade his friend good-night,
"I guess if anybody can handle 'em, he can."

It was colder in the morning, and by late afternoon

a crust was beginning to form. If the freeze kept up they would be able to travel next day.

Jim routed out the dogs before dawn and the boys loaded the two toboggans. His own cargo was supplies for his spring camp at Squaw Lake. Lindsay's was for the family, at Waba. They closed up the log house, stuck their rifles under the load lashings, and gave the teams an order to mush on.

In spite of the long thaw there was still enough snow and ice left to cover the ground, and the dogs went through the empty streets of Nakina at a trot. The loads were too heavy to permit riding the sleds, but they made a good pace down Cordingley Lake. Remembering his fall through the ice on Cranberry River, Jim prudently took a detour through the bush. That required time. When they came out to the open ice again at Poplar Lake the sun was high and the slush was melting fast. "Too bad," Jim remarked. "We'll have to lie up here overnight. I hoped we could get through today."

They struggled on as far as Lindsay's cabin and made camp. There was a wind blowing at supper time that night and the damp air had a sting in it.

"It'll freeze again tonight, all right," said Lindsay, when he came in from feeding the dogs. "Feels like a storm, though. We may get snowed in here if we don't look out."

They went to bed early. Jim woke up at three in

the morning as his habit was, and lay a moment listening to the wail of the wind outside. Then he got up and opened the door. No stars were visible but neither was it snowing. He shook Lindsay awake.

"Come on, kid," he urged. "We've got to get started before this weather hits us. You don't want to be pullin' up the High Hill carry in a snow storm."

They hurried through breakfast and packed the sleds. Then the shivering dogs were put in harness. In the windy dark the two boys stumbled out on the frozen slush of the lake and took their separate ways.

XXI

Jim pulled up the hood of his parka, for the temperature had dropped far below freezing in the night. The wind came in screaming gusts out of the north, so that he had to lean forward into it as he plodded along down the lake.

Before he had been moving an hour the first chill flakes of snow began to sting his face. "Come on, you Bruno!" he called back sharply. There were still eighteen miles to go if they were to reach the cabin at the foot of Squaw Lake. Jim could have turned back but it would mean the loss of a day or more. Except for a few well marked portages it was all lake and river trail. They couldn't get lost, even in a blinding blizzard. He decided to go on.

Five minutes later the air was so full of snow that the trees on the shore had become an indistinct shadow. Then even they were gone and there was nothing around the moving sled but a blank of whirling white.

They fought their way forward through the narrows and bore to the east down Grave Lake. The wind was quartering from the left now, and Jim kept his bearings by the sting of it on his left cheek. He looked back and found Bruno right at his heels. The big lead dog gave a soft whimper.

"What's the matter, boy?" Jim said, and stopped to see if the harness was chafing. He could feel Bruno's body tremble under his hand. Paddy was cowering between the traces, his ears cocked back, listening. Then Jim heard it. A faint sound, half lost in the bluster of the wind. The quavering, sorrowful hunting call of a wolf.

It was behind them, he thought, and on their trail. Close, too, to be heard in the teeth of that storm. Being followed by wolves was nothing new in his experience. He got his rifle off the sled. Maybe there would be chance for a shot if the snow slackened. He made sure the magazine was full and tucked the gun, still in its deerskin sheath, under his arm. "Come on, now—mush!" he growled to the dogs. "There's nothing to be afraid of."

Several times, in the next half hour, he heard that howling again. Or was his imagination playing tricks on him? Once he turned quickly and thought he saw a gray ghost shape vanish in the veil of white behind him. Impossible! He knew he couldn't see fifty yards in such a snow, and no wolf would come that close. Yet he would have sworn that something moved, back there.

Jim checked an involuntary shiver and swung forward into the storm again. Angrily he refused to glance behind, even when Bruno whined and shouldered close to his knee. Then suddenly a dark wall loomed right ahead—a narrow, wooded point, not a dozen paces away. In the few seconds it took to pull out to the left and round the spur of trees, an idea came to Jim. He turned sharply, seized Bruno's collar and jerked the team after him behind the woods. Then he sprang back to the end of the point. Breathless, he snatched the rifle out of its cover and crouched there, waiting. The wind was blowing right across the lake now—not back along the trail. Neither scent nor sound would betray his ambush. Still, wolves were wary brutes. . . .

He waited through seconds that seemed like hours, while the blood pounded in his ears and his fingers shook against the trigger guard. Why this tension had come on him he did not understand, nor did he try. It was there—a weird feeling of something strange and terrifying. He eased his cramped knees and waited. One moment there was nothing before his eyes but swirling eddies of white. The next, he was staring at a gray, moving outline—so near that he trembled—

so monstrous that his heart missed a beat. *This was the big wolf.*

Jim never remembered taking aim, but he knew that at the instant he pressed the trigger the huge beast had sensed his presence. The wolf checked, lifted its head. Then, as the bullet crashed home, it leaped straight upward.

Exultant, the boy got to his feet. The heart shot! Animals struck in the heart always went into the air. A grouse would tower in the same way. But—he rubbed his eyes and looked again—where was the furry heap he expected to see lying there? The wolf was gone!

Jim started forward, shaken. It was a scant ten yards to the place where the gray brute had been. Ten yards! Could he have missed? There was no blood in the snow—nothing but those tremendous tracks, as big as a human hand, blurred already by the sifting flakes. He looked about, stupidly, and his eye chanced to light on a depression, a few feet away to the north. More tracks. The wolf had started upwind, going in frenzied leaps, and Jim ran after. At the third set of footprints he found a great gout of crimson staining the snow. The distance between the jumps shortened.

The boy slowed his headlong pace and moved more cautiously. There was something uncanny about this pursuit. The sleet whipped blindingly into his eyes and he could see only a couple of snowshoe lengths ahead. Somewhere in that white fury—no telling how far—the biggest timber wolf in Canada was wounded, perhaps waiting for him. He clutched his rifle tight and went on, a step at a time.

As minute after minute passed, a chill of fear ran down his spine. He knew what the Indians would say. You couldn't kill a witch-wolf—a *loup-garou!* Yet he was sure the animal had been mortally hit, and there was the constant evidence of the blood-soaked trail.

It was neither sight nor sound, but a sort of intuitive sixth sense that warned him the wolf was at hand. He halted and raised the rifle, his eyes straining into the welter of flying snow. A slow stride forward. Then another. There came a momentary lull in the storm and a low gray mass took sudden shape ahead. The wolf was crouched, facing him. He saw the flattened ears—the great bloody jaws—the lips writhing back in a terrible, silent snarl.

He fired just as a new flurry of flakes swept down. But before his view was blotted out, the mighty head fell forward in the snow.

Jim was shaking all over when he reached the dead wolf. His second bullet, he found, had smashed through the skull squarely between the eyes. The first had drilled a hole back of the shoulder, and must have pierced both lungs. But what a wolf!

He stretched it out as best he could and measured the length from nose to tail tip. It was much longer than his snowshoe—nearly ten feet over all! When he gripped the hind legs and hoisted them over his shoulder the huge, gaunt body was so heavy he staggered under it. Partly carrying, partly dragging his load, he made his way back to the sled.

The dogs were still huddled in the lee of the point, out of the wind. They began barking furiously when Jim appeared with his grisly burden. Even after he had flung the carcass down in the snow, they kept their distance. The fur stood in stiff ridges along their backs, and they growled steadily, deep in their throats.

The boy paid no attention to them. He had a job to do, and lost no time in setting about it. If there had not already been a heavy load on the toboggan he would have waited till he reached camp to skin the great wolf. As it was, he knew they would have enough trouble making it through the howling storm.

He lashed the hind paws to a couple of stout branches, whetted his hunting knife and made his first cut on the inner side of the haunch.

Behind him, the dogs' growls changed suddenly to excited barking. He was in a hurry and did not look around.

"Hi, there, youngster!" rumbled a deep voice at his shoulder.

Jim's jump was almost as high as the wounded

wolf's had been. Startled, he whirled to stare up at a face in a furred parka. The man was only a pace or two away, and through the haze of flying snow he looked gigantic. As soon as he recovered from his shock of surprise, Jim recognized the newcomer.

"Sergeant MacLeish!" he gasped.

The man nodded and came a stride nearer. "So you got him," he commented. "Great day—what a brute! Wish I'd had the luck myself. Gad! Look at the size of him!"

He lifted the huge, grinning head and fingered the two-inch tusks with respect. "What's your name, son?" he asked. "Jim Vanderbeck, eh? You trap this country?"

"My brother and I," Jim replied. "He's gone on over to Wababimiga."

"So that was his track," nodded the big policeman. "They told me in Nakina I'd get to Wababimiga if I followed you boys. I picked the wrong trail and came along after you when you separated, back there. Don't know as I'm sorry, at that," he mused.

"Were—were you after the big wolf, too?" Jim asked in some awe.

"Yes," said MacLeish. "If I found him, that is." He shot a keen look at the boy's face. "Have you heard any of this Indian talk around Nakina?"

Jim nodded soberly.

"Then you know what I'm here for," the sergeant

said. "You can see why getting rid of this wolf is important. The rest of my job is over there at the Cree's camp. If I can get there before the track Indians start anything, I'll stop the trouble, of course. And if I have the wolf's hide to show them, it'll knock these fool notions out of their heads for good. Want any help with that skinning?"

"Guess not," said Jim. "I'll try an' make a decent job of it."

He went to work with his knife again and in twenty minutes the carcass was stripped. He rolled up the pelt in silence and held out the bulky bundle to the policeman.

MacLeish shook his head. "That's a valuable skin," he said, "and it's yours. I've no dogs here—just this pack on my back and my snowshoes. I'd like you to come with me. Can we make it to Wababimiga before dark?"

Jim considered. There were two possible ways. One was to go down Squaw Lake into the teeth of the storm and then strike over the hills to the north bay of Waba. The other was to head directly across and pick up the trail Lindsay had broken above the long carry.

"Yes," he answered after a moment. "We can cut south through the bush here. It may be tough going but I think we can do it."

He lashed the wolf pelt on top of his loaded toboggan and gave Bruno a friendly cuff. "Come on, now," he said, "you've got some real mushing to do. Hup, boy!"

With that he plowed ahead into the bush, ax in hand, and the tall sergeant followed the sled.

Once or twice before in his life, Jim had hiked across this same stretch of country. He knew its difficulties in a general way, but finding a path for the toboggan was far different from going through alone. Again and again he had to spend precious minutes chopping away brush and fallen trees that barred the trail. At other times he made wide detours to avoid such tangles as appeared impassable. He had no compass. If his companion carried one, the boy did not ask to see it. The storm was all he needed to give him his direction, and he knew he was on the right line as long as the wind beat at his back.

Hours passed. It must have been well past noon, though the gray, snow-filled air gave no hint of the time. They crossed a ridge of rocky hills and stumbled down the other side through beech and poplar woods. A frozen pond opened out before them as they reached the foot of the ridge. Jim halted and peered out into the white emptiness.

"I can't see the far shore clear enough to be sure," he said. "But this ought to be what we call Third Lake —just above the long carry. Wait here a bit while I scout ahead."

[244]

A moment later he shouted that he had found Lindsay's trail. When MacLeish and the dogs joined him he plowed along swiftly in the blurred furrow left by his brother's sled. From here on it was easier going. He knew the road so well he could almost have followed it blindfolded.

They struggled up the High Hill portage, pulling the sled to help the dogs, and once on the other side there was only open lake between them and Joe Leake's cabin. Jim was leading the way out of the cove from the head of Wababimiga, when he checked suddenly and stared off down the lake into the dim white of eddying flakes. When MacLeish reached him he pointed to fresh snowshoe tracks coming in from the south.

"Six or eight men," he said soberly. "Must have cut across country from the 'Jibway settlement below Nakina."

The big Scot knelt and examined the tracks, then stood quickly erect. "Come on!" he snapped. "We've no time to lose. They can't be more than a quarter of an hour ahead of us."

He jumped into the lead, his long legs setting such a pace that Jim and the dogs panted in their effort to keep up. The boy marveled at the strides he took, comparing them with those other snowshoe marks that had gone before. They must be gaining. And yet, as mile after mile went by, there was still no sign of moving figures in the blur of white ahead.

The north bay of the lake opened dimly on their left and the storm came howling down its length with staggering force. Jim lunged forward to the policeman's side. "Look!" he screamed through the wind. "They've turned into the bay. Want to sneak up on the cabin through the woods, I guess. We'll go quicker if we stay on the lake."

MacLeish nodded and they hurried on. The many snowshoe prints were gone now and only Lindsay's sled trail stretched ahead of them. At last Jim pointed to the shore. "Over there," he said. "I can't see the shack in this snow, but that's the place!"

The sergeant swung, without a word, toward the dark haze of woods. His rifle was still in its sheath as he raced across the last stretch of snow-covered ice and up the bank. Jim, urging on the dogs, was not far behind him.

"Stay here," ordered the big Mountie. He went past the cabin and on into the bush.

The boy looked about him uneasily. Except for the wail of the wind all was silent around the Cree's shack. Not even the usual yapping of dogs came from the somber log walls. The naked, shriveled carcass of a fox hung in a birch tree and swung there hideously, like an omen of evil.

He had no idea how long he waited, but it must have been more than a quarter of an hour, for his tired muscles were beginning to stiffen in the cold. Then Bruno lifted his head and whined a little, and several figures appeared at the edge of the tiny clearing. They came past the cabin and stood in a sheepish huddle near the sled. They were Indians—Ojibways from the track. Jim recognized one or two of their faces. Behind them stalked the giant police sergeant.

He faced the group, looking with grim deliberation from one to another. When at last he spoke, his words fell slowly, with a cold, cutting edge to them.

"You men have been making big fools of yourselves," he said, "about nothing. I'm going to prove it to you."

In two strides he reached the sled and seized the rolled-up wolf pelt. "Look!" he commanded. In his mittened hands the enormous skin unfolded and he held it high in front of him, the gray brush trailing on the ground.

"Tell me," he snapped. "Is it the big wolf?"

A chorus of astonished grunts answered him. One of the Indians stepped forward timidly and touched the huge, bloody head. "Yes," he muttered in fear.

"You see?" demanded MacLeish inexorably. "The big wolf is dead. This boy killed him. And you, who come here with guns to make trouble—do you know you are breaking the law of the Dominion?"

His deep voice rumbled the words like thunder, and the Indians were shaking in their moccasins. Jim heard the faint creak of a leather hinge behind him. Turning quickly he saw that the cabin door had opened and closed again. Joe Leake was standing there with a rifle gripped in his hands, a look of fear and hatred on his face. He made no sound, but the sergeant saw the eyes of the Indians shift and glanced over his shoulder.

"Put that gun down," he said sternly. The Cree hesitated a second, then obeyed.

"Is your name Joe Leake?" asked MacLeish.

The Indian nodded slowly.

"Tell your woman to come out. Tell her not to be afraid. I am here to take care of you."

At the words he pulled back the opening of his parka so that the red tunic showed underneath. The Cree stared, awe-struck, then shook his head.

"Woman gone," he croaked.

"Where? Tell me—where did she go?"

"No tell," the Indian answered, with a shrug of his shoulders. "Take-um dogs, small papoose, go las' night."

There was a superstitious muttering among the Ojibways, but MacLeish silenced them with a hard glance. He left off questioning the Cree and took a long step toward them.

"Listen to me," he said harshly, "and remember what I tell you now. You have broken the law. But for this one time I will not punish you. Go home to

Nakina. Tell your people you are fools. Tell them you have seen the skin of the big wolf. He will trouble you no more. And you make no more trouble. Now go!"

As he snapped out the last words, they turned with hanging heads and left the clearing. Silently, in single file, they took the trail up the lake.

"All right, Joe Leake," said MacLeish. "They won't come back again. Tell me," he asked curiously, "your wife's in there, isn't she?"

The Indian's face was stubbornly set. He shook his head again. "Woman gone," was all he would say.

"Okay," frowned the policeman. "Have it your way. You don't seem much worried about her, though."

He turned to Jim. "Well, boy," he smiled, "many thanks. Where are you camping tonight? It'll be getting dusk pretty soon and I don't feel much like hiking back to town."

"You don't have to," Jim grinned delightedly. "My folks live right down the lake a couple o' miles. I know they'll be glad to put you up."

He roused the tired dogs and led the way out on the ice. The snow had practically stopped falling now, and the wind had slackened in force. They stayed in the lee of the wooded shore and plodded along through drifts a foot and more in depth.

The sergeant pulled up abreast of his guide. "Sorry

that woman wasn't around," he mused. "I wanted to show 'em that witch idea was so much tommyrot. Now I suppose they'll say her spirit departed when you shot the wolf, or something of the kind."

He chuckled as he said it, but the words sent a shiver through Jim. "G—gosh!" he stuttered. "I sure would hate to think that!"

"Well, don't let it worry you," laughed the big Mountie.

There was a light in the window of the cabin when they pulled into the home cove. Jim cupped his mittened hands and sent a loud halloo echoing through the clearing. Dogs began to bark in the kennels and Pat and Bruno gave deep-tongued answer. Lindsay's broad shoulders appeared in the doorway.

"Well, for the love of—" he began. "Dad! Look who's here!"

Jim stuck his snowshoes up in front of the team and ushered Sergeant MacLeish into the cabin. The family made a welcoming knot around them while the boy was introducing his big friend.

"And who's that?" asked the sergeant looking over their heads toward the far corner of the room. Jim followed his glance. There, squatted on one of the beds, he saw Joe Leake's Eskimo squaw calmly nursing a tiny copper-skinned papoose.

Musk Rat

XXII

"She came by here last night," Ida explained. "Stopped and wanted to borrow a few matches. She can't talk any English to speak of, but she makes out with sign language. Near as we can figure she was starting for Hudson Bay—all alone with the baby and a team of dogs. Dad said it was coming on to snow and wouldn't let her go on."

The woman sat there smiling at them all, a trustful look in her slanting black eyes.

"Well," said Sergeant MacLeish, "if there's any way to let her know, it ought to be safe for her to go home now. We've chased those track Indians back to Nakina."

"Let me talk to her," Mrs. Vanderbeck offered.

"We sort of understand each other. You men folks take off your things an' get 'em dried out. Supper'll be ready in a few minutes."

Jim took the dogs back to the kennels and unloaded the sled. While he was still outside, his brother joined him. "I'm goin' to harness her team," Lindsay said. "Ma got it over to her that she'll be all right at home an' she's startin' right away. Gee, boy! Wish I'd been with you when the big wolf came along! MacLeish was tellin' us about it."

The giant Scotchman spent the night with them and they were sorry to see him go in the morning. Naturally a man of few words, he had unbent in the cordial atmosphere of the Vanderbeck household and entertained them with yarn after yarn.

He shook Jim's hand at parting, with a grip that made the boy wince. "They ought to pay you a double bounty on that wolf," he grinned. "Killing him was worth a lot to the Government. If you're willing to sell the pelt, I'd like to recommend to the officials in Ottawa or Toronto that they have it mounted and made part of the permanent exhibit."

"I was planning to make a rug out of it," said Jim, flushing with pleasure. "But if the Government wants it—gee! That would be swell, wouldn't it!"

The sun was bright that morning and the temperature was rising rapidly. When MacLeish had left, Jim set about repacking his toboggan.

"It'll be thawing by noon," he told the family. "I'll have to strike out for Squaw Lake right away, if I want to have any supplies in camp this spring."

He hitched up Bruno and Pat and put on his long snowshoes. In ten minutes he was breaking trail northward on the Porcupine Lake route. From Porcupine he swung left toward the foot of Squaw, and by the time the snow had begun to melt he was on the long south cove of the lake.

When Jim reached camp he lost no time in unpacking his spring provisions and getting to work on the wolf skin. There was hardly any fat on the inside of the huge pelt, but he scraped it carefully, removing every shred of flesh. He was glad now that he had not taken time to cut off the great dangling paws when he stripped the carcass. He skinned them now, taking out the bones as far as the toes and fleshing the thin, tough hide of the legs. Finally he stretched the pelt over an immense frame of birch. It was a job that took him till late in the evening, but when he surveyed his handiwork he was well pleased.

The morning was well advanced when he finished breakfast next day. It was thawing already, and too soft to travel with the dogs. However, he was able to get around fairly well on snowshoes, and in the afternoon he started out to follow up a brook that flowed into the lake near his camp.

After three or four miles the course of the little

stream led him to a swampy muskeg pond. The surface looked treacherous. He skirted around it through the bush and continued up the inlet on the other side. And suddenly he saw open water before him. It came as a shock in the middle of that snowbound landscape —a dark pool rippling in the breeze, with tiny curls and eddies of steam rising from its surface.

Jim went closer and knelt beside it. He took off his mitten and put his hand in the water. To his amazement it was warm—almost hot. The pool was nearly twenty feet across and round in shape. Bending down, he could see white sand bubbling at the bottom—a warm spring!

Looking around him, the boy found hundreds of tracks mingling in the snow. Mink, otter, fisher and fox; rabbit, weasel, and even deer had used the spring as a drinking place. For him this discovery was what finding a vein of pure gold would be to a prospector. He would trap the place next winter. In the meantime he wanted to stake his claim. With the point of his knife he dug a deep "J. V." in the trunk of the nearest large tree. That would warn anyone who came after him that he had a prior right to the trapping there.

Jim spent two more days exploring the country around the camp. Very early on the morning of the 20th of April he harnessed the dogs and set out for Wababimiga. The weather had been so warm that he expected open water in the lakes and rivers soon, and he wanted to be ready to begin setting muskrat traps as early as possible. Ida was to come with him, to cook and help with the trapping.

When he reached the family's camp he found Mary had already gone to join Lindsay at Poplar, and his older sister had her knapsack all packed, awaiting his arrival. They would have started back next morning, but it snowed and rained all day and kept them housebound. Then the weather turned in the night. There was a frozen crust that crunched under their snowshoes when they left the clearing at daybreak. With them they took only one dog—old Bruno—for company. He had no sled to pull, but the habit was so strong that he still plodded along behind them, following the trail they broke.

Ida had never seen the line camp on Squaw Lake. "My goodness, what an untidy mess!" she exclaimed when Jim threw open the door. "I don't see how you men folks live, when you're off by yourselves like this, all winter!"

"What's the matter with it?" asked Jim in surprise. "I picked things up special, just before I came away."

Ida laughed. "Well," she said, "I don't suppose it would bother a man, but wait till I get through straightening up. I bet you'll notice the difference. Go cut me some alder switches right off. No—I'm not going to spank you. I want to do some sweeping."

Jim tied a bunch of alder withes together on the end of a stick and made a passable broom. As he watched his sister energetically brushing up the dirt floor, an idea came to him. He said nothing to Ida about it, but before he turned in for the night he sharpened his ax.

Breakfast the next morning tasted better than usual, he had to admit. Ida certainly knew how to make good coffee. When he had cleaned up the last of the flapjacks, he put on his outdoor clothes.

"I'll be back for lunch," he told her. "Going up back in the bush an' cut some wood."

That was true enough, though, if she had noticed the huge pile of firewood beside the cabin, she must have thought it an unnecessary chore.

Jim selected a clump of tall, straight spruces and began operations. He felled and trimmed half a dozen of them, split them with wedges, and began smoothing the flat sides with his ax. When they were level enough to suit him, he trimmed off an inch or two of the round surface and straightened the split edges. By night he had some fairly presentable hewn lumber, a foot wide and four or five inches thick.

That evening, while Ida was outside feeding the dog, Jim got a long piece of string out of his possible-sack and measured the length and breadth of the cabin floor. She came in before he expected her and caught him at it.

"So that's what you've been up to!" she laughed. "A grand idea, too, Jim. When do you want to begin putting it in? I'll help you move things."

"Shucks!" he said. "I was going to send you off on an expedition somewhere an' surprise you. Still, I guess you can be some help, at that. I'll cut off the planks the right length, an' we'll haul 'em down here tomorrow."

When the new puncheon floor was in, the place really began to look neat and comfortable. But Jim didn't stop with the floor. While the carpentering spell was on him, he built new table shelves, a cupboard for Ida's dishes, and a chair that could be sat in without causing curvature of the spine.

These operations occupied Jim's time for several days. But when they were finished he began to grow restless. He took a trip up to Sucker Lake hoping to find open water. The ice was rotting fast but there was no chance to set traps. Down Squaw River the same conditions prevailed. Only the rapids and a few patches in the middle of the stream were clear.

Day after day, the spring sun shone warm and the drifts melted in the woods. Every night there was a gurgle of running water, seeping down from the high ground to swell the brooks. One bright blue morning Ida called her brother to look at a great flock of ducks flying north. They were too high for him to distinguish what kind they were, but the sound of their quacking came thin and eerie out of the sky.

Jim wanted action at once. "See here," he said, pointing to the calendar Lindsay had left on the wall. "It's the first day of May. Plenty late to start spring trapping. And those ducks know there's open water somewhere up here. Come on—let's find it!"

He loaded his pack with a dozen traps and enough food to make lunch. As an afterthought he took a light, jointed rod, and stuck a trout fly or two in his hat brim.

Four or five miles down the Squaw they came to a long reach where the ice was entirely gone. It was still water, shoaling into marshy grass along the banks. Along the far shore a V-shaped ripple was moving swiftly upstream.

"Look at that!" breathed Jim ecstatically. "There goes a rat now!"

He laid out his traps on the snowy bank and started operations. He had put on his mukluks that morning. They were high moccasins of sealskin, made somewhere north on Hudson Bay. Worn for spring trapping, they were always warm and completely waterproof. The only precaution necessary with mukluks was to keep them from freezing. Exposed to too low temperatures the soft hide grew brittle and cracked.

Jim waded into the shallows among the dead grass stems, and found a drift log lying with one end out of water. Just at the edge, where the ripples lapped it, he cut a notch wide enough to hold a No. 1 trap, and deep enough so that the pan would be level with the surface of the log. The end of the chain was fastened to the wood with a common fence staple and the set was ready.

A muskrat trap needs no bait. Its success depends on placing it where the animal will step into it. In the first days of open water, every rat is looking for logs, fallen trees or rocks where he can crawl out and sun himself, and Jim took advantage of all the natural spots of this kind along the shore when he set his traps. At one or two places he felled a poplar so that the trunk would lie half in the water, and put the trap in a notch, as he had on the drift log.

When all the sets had been made, they still had an hour or two before lunch.

"How about going up to the foot of the rapid," the boy suggested, "an' finding out if the fish are hungry. Let's see—they oughtn't to be very fussy this time o' year. Guess I'll try a spinner with a Par Belle fly."

He put his rod together and tied on the leader. "Here goes!" he called to Ida. "First cast o' the season!"

The line sang out sweetly and the fly dropped with a tempting flicker at the edge of the eddy. It had drifted only a yard or two when a big trout struck with a ravenous rush. The battle lasted five minutes but the fish was too securely hooked to need much finesse. Ida was ready with the landing net.

"Two-pounder," panted Jim, as the gleaming trout thrashed on the bank. "That's a good start. Here— you try a cast."

When they lighted the luncheon fire there were five fish ready for the pan. And no royal feast ever tasted better than those fresh trout after a winter of dried moose meat and bacon.

On the return trip to camp they saw many cakes of rotten ice washing down the rapids. It was coming out of the lake fast, melting and breaking away under the May sun.

"That means we can use the canoes by tomorrow, if the weather stays warm," Jim told his sister. "Gee, it'll feel good to swing a paddle again!"

There was no freeze that night and, after the mist cleared, no cloud in the sky next morning. Ida helped Jim launch the canoe which was on a rack behind the camp. They poled down the fast water to a new stretch of open river below, and set more traps before lunchtime. Coming back, with the white rush of the rapids to fight, Jim found his poling muscles woefully stiff from lack of use. It was always so in the first day or two of canoe travel. He knew he would limber up and recover his skill before the week was out.

That afternoon he walked up the brook to Sucker

Lake. To his joy there were large patches of open water offshore, and he began at once to construct a number of rat-rafts. They were made of two good-sized logs, deeply notched at the ends. A pair of lighter sticks nailed crosswise, held them in position, and a pole driven into the mud of the lake bottom kept them from floating away. Then a trap was set in each notch.

Heavy clouds had gathered before Jim finished building the last of his four rafts. A low grumble of thunder rolled down across the bush. Hastily the boy placed the final trap and started for home. The storm held off until he was almost in sight of the cabin, and then with a roar like artillery fire it let loose in earnest. He raced to the door and entered, with water sluicing off his hat and shoulders. Ida was humming cheerfully as she got supper.

"Well!" she grinned at him. "I do believe it's raining."

The thunder ripped and bellowed through the woods and the deluge shook the roof poles.

"Raining!" Jim snorted, when he could make himself heard. "It's pouring pitchforks! An' look at that lightning! Well, I guess it proves that spring's really here!"

Beaver

XXIII

IF there had been any doubts remaining as to the arrival of spring in the Northland, the next few days would have dispelled them. Warm winds blew from the southeast, bringing birds in ever-increasing flocks. Pintails and green-winged teal dotted the coves almost as soon as the mushy ice had drifted out. Wood ducks and sawbills, butter-balls and golden-eyes splashed and swam among the reeds. Back along the sun-drenched woods trails, black and white warblers were fifing their shrill song, and before many days they were followed by other tiny singers—sweet-voiced hermit thrushes and rusty-coated fox sparrows.

The winter snowbanks dwindled magically, till

only a few pitted remnants of white remained in the shadow of the spruce thickets. Buds began to crack their frost-proof shells on the hardwood trees. And every day at noon it was so hot that Jim and Ida shed their mackinaws and sweaters. When spring finally reaches the Hudson Bay slope, it comes with a rush.

The business of rat-trapping went on apace. Jim had set up his entire line by the end of the first week in May, and he went over it every two days. It was nothing unusual to take ten or twelve muskrats out of the traps between dawn and sunset. This meant that he had to spend all his spare time skinning and stretching the pelts. Having Ida to keep house for him was a great help. She cooked all the meals, cut wood for the fire, and was always ready to take a hand with the skinning or to catch a trout for supper.

The open season on muskrat ended May 21st. In an ordinary spring the trapping was expected to yield a hundred and fifty skins or more. This year the water had opened so late that Jim was cheated of at least ten days, and he had hardly hoped for a catch of more than a hundred. On the 20th he counted his pelts and found there were ninety-two already in the pile.

"Today's the last day," he told Ida at breakfast. "Come along with me and bring me luck. We'll go up Sucker Lake and come back down Squaw."

They got off early and by nine o'clock were launch-

ing the canoe on Sucker Lake. There was nothing in
the first half dozen traps which Jim picked up. Then,
in quick succession, he found two in bank sets and
one on a raft. From that point on it seemed as if all
the rats in Thunder Bay District had swarmed to the
boy's lures. He lost count before they reached Squaw
Lake, but he knew the sack that held them was almost
as heavy as the jingling load of sprung traps.

When they paddled to shore at the home cabin and
emptied the bag he found there were twenty-two
prime pelts—a day's record catch. It was nearly eleven
o'clock that night when the last skin was on the
stretchers.

*   *   *   *

They loaded all the skins, the dog and a few provisions into the canoe next morning, and went up the
lake to meet Lindsay and Mary. They were at their
camp when Jim and Ida arrived. As it was too late
in the day to start for Waba, the quartet stayed at
Poplar Lake overnight. It was a merry party. The
boys played their mouth organs, the girls sang and
made candy, and they all wound up with a few hands
of bridge before bedtime.

As soon as breakfast was finished they were off,
racing their canoes down the thoroughfares and
through the chain of lakes to the long carry. By midafternoon they were paddling down the blue length

of Wababimiga. Joe Leake's squaw and three or four
of her dusky youngsters waved a friendly greeting
from the shore as they went by. Then they were
rounding the last island and heading for the home
cove.

Their arrival was expected, as they could see from
the small Canadian flag waving from the end of the
landing dock. Mr. and Mrs. Vanderbeck came down
the trail to meet them, laughing, asking questions, exclaiming over the size of the bales of skins the boys
took out of the canoes.

There was a special feast prepared that night in
honor of the returning trappers. Speckled trout and
fried potatoes, toothsome hot biscuits and a huge blueberry pie. When the dishes were done and the dogs
fed, they sat around the lamp and swapped yarns
about all that had happened since they had last been
together.

Big Lindsay lighted his pipe and sat in the corner,
scribbling figures on a piece of paper. "A pretty good
year after all," he said at length "—thanks to you
boys. The winter furs and wolf bounties brought in
$910. And the rats helped, too. You got a hundred an'
fourteen, didn't you, Jim? And Lindsay caught
eighty. I set a few traps an' I believe my pelts'll run
to about twenty-five or six. Say two-twenty alto-
gether. If the price holds up that'll make $275. With
the bounty on Jim's big wolf, we'll take in better than

$1200 for the season."

"Don't forget what the skin of the big wolf'll bring," Jim put in. "He ought to be worth thirty-five or forty dollars."

His father smiled and shook his head. "We won't count that in the family cash," he said. "I reckon that money belongs to you, son. An' that reminds me. Emile brought us some mail from town an' I've got a surprise for you."

He handed the boy a long, official-looking envelope. "Read it aloud," he suggested.

Astonished, Jim drew out a letter with the Provincial Seal at the top. He began to read:

Mr. James Vanderbeck,
Nakina, Ontario
Dear Sir:

We have learned, through Sergt. MacLeish, R.C.M.P., of your recent exploit in killing a large timber wolf which had been terrorizing the district near Nakina. We understand from Sergt. MacLeish that this wolf is an exceptionally large specimen and that you have preserved the skin.

While no reward had been posted for the capture of the wolf, continued depredations would undoubtedly have made one advisable, and we would like to see you properly recompensed for ridding Ontario of such a pest. We are, therefore, prepared to offer you $250 for the skin if it is in such condition that it can be mounted.

This, of course, will not prevent you from collecting the usual bounty of $25 from the local warden. If you wish to accept the above offer, kindly forward the skin to this office by express at your early convenience.

Please accept our sincere appreciation and thanks for settling a difficulty which might have developed troublesome consequences if it had been allowed to continue.

Yours very truly,

Department of Game and Fisheries

Province of Ontario

Jim drew a long breath and beamed on the assembled company.

"Gosh!" he murmured, overcome by the liberality of the offer. "Two hundred an' fifty dollars! An' they're going to have him mounted. Lindsay, you an' I'll sure have to take that trip to Toronto we've talked about. We'll see the ol' wolf standin' up there as big as life!"

Their father leaned back, puffing contentedly on his dark old briar.

"Got some more letters in the mail," he announced. "Party comin' up from Chicago for the fishin', first week in June. We'll just about have time to move back to Nakina an' get our outfits ready.

"Then there are three or four booked up for the moose season—regulars mostly. An' some friends o'

Mr. Warren's want to take a three-weeks' canoe trip to the Albany, some time in August. It's not like boom times, but there'll be enough to keep us busy an' pay expenses. I've asked Emile an' the Lagarde boys to guide for us again."

*   *   *   *

The family prepared for bed, and Jim stole out alone into the clearing in front of the cabin. A soft spring wind ruffled the spruce boughs and stars burned brightly overhead in the velvet night. He heard a fox bark in the bush to the north. From far across the lake came the weird, wild laughter of a loon. Close by, at the edge of the cove, a feeding moose splashed among the lily stems.

Jim was happy. His heart was full. Tomorrow they would be packing for the return to town, and a busy summer stretched ahead. But nothing could take away from him the secret thrill of this night. Silently he lifted his arms in a salute to his beloved woods, then turned and went into the cabin.

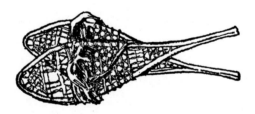

Printed in the United States
45655LVS00002B/583-591